# ENDOW

## A BLOOD INHERITANCE NOVEL

## M. AINIHI

M. AINIHI

# Endow

*A Blood Inheritance Novel*

First published by M. Ainihi 2020

Copyright © 2020 by M. Ainihi

All rights reserved. No part of this publication may be reproduced, stored or transmitted in any form or by any means, electronic, mechanical, photocopying, recording, scanning, or otherwise without written permission from the publisher. It is illegal to copy this book, post it to a website, or distribute it by any other means without permission.

This novel is entirely a work of fiction. The names, characters and incidents portrayed in it are the work of the author's imagination. Any resemblance to actual persons, living or dead, events or localities is entirely coincidental.

M. Ainihi asserts the moral right to be identified as the author of this work.

M. Ainihi has no responsibility for the persistence or accuracy of URLs for external or third-party Internet Websites referred to in this publication and does not guarantee that any content on such Websites is, or will remain, accurate or appropriate.

Designations used by companies to distinguish their products are often claimed as trademarks. All brand names and product names used in this book and on its cover are trade names, service marks, trademarks and registered trademarks of their respective owners. The publishers and the book are not associated with any product or vendor mentioned in this book. None of the companies referenced within the book have endorsed the book.

First edition

ISBN: 978-0-9993514-9-9

Editing by Allister Thompson
Illustration by Tauseef Ahmed
Cover art by rebecacover

This book was professionally typeset on Reedsy.
Find out more at reedsy.com

*Dedicated to my
Ladybug
as she fights to find her way*

# Contents

| | | |
|---|---|---|
| 1 | Amanda - Arrival | 1 |
| 2 | Emily - White Rabbit | 6 |
| 3 | Kiami - The Unique Youngling | 13 |
| 4 | Amanda - Enigma | 25 |
| 5 | Emily - Angst | 28 |
| 6 | Amanda - Manipulation | 32 |
| 7 | Kiami - Sandcastle | 35 |
| 8 | Emily - Jinn Village | 46 |
| 9 | Amanda - Lair | 53 |
| 10 | Kiami - Turbulence | 63 |
| 11 | Emily - Weather Patterns | 67 |
| 12 | Emily - Stormwich | 74 |
| 13 | Amanda - Aeron | 84 |
| 14 | Emily - Pressure | 94 |
| 15 | Amanda - The Confession | 99 |
| 16 | Kiami - Truth Hurts | 103 |
| 17 | Emily - Vanishing Act | 107 |
| 18 | Amanda - Etzion | 113 |
| 19 | Kiami - The Great Pretender | 120 |
| 20 | Amanda - Fight Song | 127 |
| 21 | Emily - A Real Hoot | 133 |
| 22 | Amanda - Wrong Turn | 143 |
| 23 | Emily - Cry Wolf | 152 |
| 24 | Kiami - Right Track | 157 |

| | | |
|---|---|---|
| 25 | Emily – Bloise | 169 |
| 26 | Amanda – Hara Berezaiti | 186 |
| 27 | Kiami – Going Hunting | 193 |
| 28 | Emily – Of Talismans and Tales | 197 |
| 29 | Amanda – The Climb | 207 |
| 30 | Kiami – Long Trip Down | 214 |
| 31 | Amanda – Riverside | 222 |
| 32 | Kiami – Whispers | 229 |
| 33 | Emily – Intuition | 236 |
| 34 | Amanda – Downward Spiral | 240 |
| 35 | Kiami – Waiting Game | 244 |
| 36 | Amanda – The Unexpected | 246 |
| 37 | Emily – Powerless | 264 |
| 38 | Amanda – Dream on | 270 |
| 39 | Amanda – Collapse | 276 |
| 40 | Kiami – Shaken | 280 |
| 41 | Emily – Mission Statement | 284 |
| *About the Author* | | 289 |
| *Also by M. Ainihi* | | 290 |

# 1

## Amanda - Arrival

Travel with the help of her shadow magic seemed to be harder on the others than on her. At least, that's what Amanda had thought when they first arrived at the edge of the woods that encircled Justin's home. The trio around her looked haggard and pale.

Justin stared wide-eyed and slack-jawed in her direction, even after Emily stood, hunched over, pulling her arms taut across her stomach. Only Kiami rushed to her side, trying to help her stay on her feet as she began to heave and retch.

Of course, traveling hadn't been the only cause of their worn appearance. They hadn't taken much time to recover from the battle with URD before leaving the Arcane realm.

She looked down at her hand, which still firmly grasped the staff that had aided in harnessing her powers. Without it, she couldn't have hoped to defeat the monstrous being that had threatened them.

She recalled how the branch had sprung to life with magic, growing, twisting, and shaping itself around her gem.

Its appearance had changed significantly since they fought the creature. Its coloring had dulled, and the new growth of leaves had fallen off. It no longer resembled a living thing, as it had after it was first created.

Disconcerted by its modified, lifeless appearance, she let it fall to the ground at her feet. She seemed to affect everything and everyone she came into contact with in this way, as if death followed close behind her at every step, perhaps hiding within the very shadows from which her blood heritage allowed her to draw power.

Amanda folded her arms across her chest and looked up into the sky, wondering if she was being gullible in thinking that things could be any different with their help.

Maybe, deep down, she was still the same naïve girl she had been since the start.

Unusual clusters of coloring dappled the sky, and Amanda had the sudden desire to turn tail and run. She sighed wearily, the anxious energy draining from her.

She couldn't allow her friends' sacrifices to be in vain.

Amanda kept her face turned skyward as Justin's eyes continued to burn through her. Even though she had given in and returned with them to the human realm, as he had desired, there was no softness in his gaze. It was a look that conveyed a bubbling hatred for her. Perhaps even disgust.

She cursed under her breath. She should have known leaving the Arcane realm with them wouldn't change his opinion of her. She had seen the tight look in his eyes when Emily had insisted she return to the human realm with them, and she had followed his gaze as he snuck a glance at Kiami. His eyes were weary when he looked away from her eager, smiling form, but he had said nothing as he used his palm to wipe the beads of anxious sweat from his forehead, then across his pantleg.

She could see the shape of the girls shuffle by, just a blurry outline caught in her peripheral vision. Still, she refused to back down and give him the satisfaction of acknowledgment.

She had already guessed it was Justin's eyes she had seen through during her last vision.

She breathed in sharply. The air felt lighter, sweeter than she remembered.

It had been a while since she had spent any real time in the human realm, even longer since she had physically entered a human home, although she knew what to expect when she went inside.

The image of the first floor was still crisp in her mind. The winding staircase, the L-shaped sofa, the fireplace, and mantle. She even had a glimpse of the kitchen during the episode before she had been forced out of his head.

Of the many visions she had been thrust into in the past, no one before

Justin had ever given an inkling that they had felt her as a passenger.

How he was connected to her and the others, she wasn't yet sure. In fact, if he was truly one of them, the discovery could ruin her entire hypothesis. That is, unless he was keeping something from them, which Amanda expected might just be the case.

Right now, he barely seemed to possess jinn abilities at all, let alone some extraordinary power like Kiami's song or the healing talent of Emily.

She wondered if he had realized it was her that had invaded his mind. Surely, he would have told the others if he had, and they had not indicated to her that they suspected anything of the sort.

She felt a breeze brush past her exposed arms, and as the sound of the door slamming shut hit her ears, she allowed her shoulders to slump. He had finally abandoned his post.

From the moment she found Erol's prison in the woods, all that she had gone through to get here swirled in her head.

Her father's possession, Erol's death, Aden's friendship and the loss of his life. She believed something inside of her had been broken by the experiences, and she wasn't sure saving the world would make her feel better. She couldn't even be sure the world really needed saving.

As powerful as she was, she knew her own insecurities would stop her from ever being able to lead the others to the truth. Just as Justin would never trust her, she wasn't sure she could ever place her own trust in the jinn that lived here.

For them to be successful, she would need to convince one of the others to lead them. She wondered who the best option would be.

Although Kiami was just as strong, if not stronger than Amanda herself, Amanda couldn't help but feel that Kiami's optimistic approach to everything would make her a poor choice. And of course, there was the fact still buried deep that Amanda had banished Kiami's Aunt Jacqueline to the jinn realm. Amanda wasn't sure how she would react to that, if and when she found out.

The extent of Kiami's feelings toward Jacqueline were hard for Amanda to gauge, although her guardian had hurt Kiami with the cruel accusations she had made. Amanda knew she still worried and cared for the jinni. It would be impossible to anticipate her reaction.

Justin was as of yet unaware of what Amanda suspected lay dormant inside of him, but even if his powers suddenly manifested to their full potential, he was a wild card in every way.

That left Emily to take the reins. Her cautious consideration could be just what they needed. Unlike herself, Amanda had noticed that Emily had a way of evaluating every aspect of a problem rather than rushing head-first into it.

# 2

# Emily - White Rabbit

Emily flinched at the loud bang the door made when it shut. She looked up at Kiami and shook her head just as a gust of wind blew her hair back from her face. She didn't need to see Justin to know it was him rushing by.

"I will never get used to that." Her eyes darted around the kitchen. "Where's Amanda?"

"Still outside." Kiami had sat at the small dining room table, her chin resting on the palm of her hand and her elbow squarely on the surface. "Are you feeling better?"

Emily chewed at her lip and nodded. She didn't want Kiami to worry. "I'm going to go get her." She tried to swallow back the intense nausea that still lingered in the pit of her stomach as she reached for the door handle.

She hesitated and glanced back at Kiami. It hadn't just been the journey that had caused her to hunch over as her stomach revolted.

Even though she didn't think Amanda would have minded her bringing the strange wooden book back with her, she had hidden it beneath her layers of shirts.

Since the book itself was written in a strange language, she hadn't wanted anyone to question her about her choice. She knew the note she had found folded within its pages was private, and she didn't want Amanda to remember that she had put it there.

On their journey back from the Arcane realm, it had almost slipped from beneath its hiding place, and she had bent over to keep it from falling out on their arrival in the human realm.

When Kiami had left her in the bathroom after helping her up the stairs, she had slipped the book into the cabinet under the sink.

It had seemed like a safe spot to stow it until she could take it back to her home.

She stepped out into the sunlight and looked around. Amanda's staff rested on the ground near her feet as she stared up into the sky.

Surprised to see Amanda still standing in the same spot they had left her in, Emily mimicked her stance as she followed her gaze, squinting at the patchwork of colors overhead. They seemed to be rapidly spreading out and connecting like a poorly sewn quilt. It appeared as if they would soon completely overtake the sky's normally blue hue.

"It looks funny."

"What's that?" Emily asked, startled by the sudden remark.

"Have you ever seen the sky look like that, Em?"

She shook her head and reached for Amanda's hand. "I think you should come inside."

As Amanda turned her gaze toward her, goosebumps prickled on her arms.

"What am I doing here, Emily?"

Like her, Amanda's eyes had an unnatural coloring, except instead of the purple flecks that dotted her irises, Amanda's showed a deep red.

Emily wondered if the coloring was what caused them to have such a haunted look. "I am hoping we will find out when we speak with the townspeople."

Amanda cocked her eyebrows and placed her hands onto her hips. "Are you? From what I understand, the only jinni that could help me was Aden, and he is not coming back."

"Let's talk about this inside."

"Do you really think that Justin wants to listen to me? I see the way he looks at me and we have barely even spoken."

"Aden believed in you."

She paused as Amanda cast her gaze down to the ground, and she wondered if she would ever be ready to tell them what had happened to him. She placed her hand on Amanda's shoulder and looked into her eyes. "Justin's been through his own share of heartache, you know. I am not excusing his behavior, but I think he has his reasons..." *He just hasn't told me all of them yet,* she thought as she trailed off.

Now that she had a moment to reflect on it, she realized that his behavior had begun to undergo minor changes ever since the car accident. Only someone that knew him would have noticed.

It had been subtle, the difference in his mood, and she couldn't help but wonder if the event had jarred something loose, maybe a memory of his accident with his parents.

She chewed at her bottom lip as she scrutinized her memory. A lot of time had passed since then. She wondered if her own worry and excitement had clouded over the small changes she now realized had been happening even before Amanda or Kiami had been present.

She returned her focus to Amanda, who now seemed to be looking through her at the house, lost in her own thoughts. "We have all been through something, and we each deal with it in our own way."

Emily's statement seemed to snap Amanda back from wherever her mind had wandered, and she raised one of her eyebrows as she responded, "You seem to be handling everything in a rational way."

Emily shook her head. "Don't mistake my calmness as a sign that I am ready to take on more. It's exhaustion, pure and simple. I think we all need to focus on getting some rest."

She could hear Amanda whisper, "Good luck with that," as she reached down to retrieve her discarded staff, but she shook it off.

Even with the strange occurrences that had been happening before their journey to the human realm, Emily felt safer here than anywhere else she had ever traveled or lived.

Emily threw one last uneasy glance toward the sky before heading for the cover of the house.

She watched Amanda closely as she propped her staff by the door before making her way over the threshold of Justin's home. As if Amanda could sense the question that played on her lips, she looked down at her and said, "I have no desire to make Justin more uncomfortable than he is." She smirked. "Yet."

Emily couldn't help but stare back in dismay as Amanda pushed past her, straight through the kitchen and into the sitting room.

She hurried to follow, almost bumping into her at the bottom of the spiral staircase that jutted out behind the L-shaped sofa. "You shouldn't make jokes like that."

Amanda snickered. "I doubt it much matters what I say or do around Justin. His mind is already made up." She motioned to the staircase. "Is that where Justin and Kiami are?"

Emily shrugged. "Kiami must have gone up after I went outside to get you." She thought of the letter she had found in the castle library and wondered if she should bring it up now to Amanda while Justin was preoccupied...

Before she could summon the courage, Kiami appeared, descending the stairs on such light feet that Emily never would have heard her or known she was coming if she hadn't been watching.

"He won't answer the door. I think I should go see what he's doing."

Amanda said, "I thought you decided that you didn't like spying, Kiami."

"I wasn't spying — I mean, I'm worried about him. I want to help him."

Emily addressed Amanda. "Is it really spying if I am trying to help him? What he's going through, we caused."

"You mean *I* caused," Amanda interjected.

"No. That's not what I said. I don't regret following Aden into the Arcane realm, and I don't regret coming here when you asked me to."

"I almost killed you."

Emily stared at the two girls, not sure what to say.

Amanda's voice rose a notch with each declaration, but Kiami's stayed firm and level as she continued.

"You saved us from URD, we couldn't have done it alone. We wouldn't have known where to start."

"Well, you wouldn't have been there at all if you hadn't been chasing after me!" Amanda glanced back and forth between them before she lowered herself slowly onto the step. "I couldn't save Aden."

It was what they had expected, but hearing her say it made Emily's heart sink. He had been trying to help because he cared for Amanda, and she could tell that it was eating her up inside.

Kiami squeezed in beside her, placing an arm around her shoulders.

This time it felt right, and Emily placed her hand on Amanda's knee. "Why don't you tell the two of us what happened to Aden."

"Aden pulled me to the dream realm. He thought it would be safer to talk to me there. But he wasn't safe. Abaddon was there, and it was all my fault." Amanda looked up, an intense emotion burning in her eyes. "I should have told him about Abaddon. He had been coming to me in my dreams for some time. But I thought if he didn't know, he would be safer."

Emily recognized the name as the one URD had used for its master. "You defeated it?"

"Not before Aden sacrificed his own life to save mine. And for what? Everyone that gets involved with me is doomed sooner or later."

Kiami spoke up. "You know our lives haven't been normal since long before we met you."

Emily glanced over at Kiami; her silver streaked hair shimmered in the lighting above the stairs. Likewise, she realized the strange silvery sheen that ran over Kiami's eyes was just as startling as the red hue of Amanda's.

She tugged at her curls, pulling them one at a time into her line of sight until a springy purple one appeared. She wondered if these strange features could tell them anything, and made a mental note to find out more about when the girls had first noticed they had these differences.

A resounding thud echoed from the second story of the house, followed by the rattling and crashing of smaller objects. Emily looked up the staircase in alarm.

Kiami rose to her feet. "Should I..."

"Go on, Kiami. You don't need our permission, or does she?" Amanda looked questioningly up at Emily.

"If you are insinuating that I'm in charge, you're crazy. We work together as a team."

Amanda pulled herself to her feet and leaned against the rail of the staircase. "Someone has to be in charge."

"Who says?"

Kiami's hand gripped Emily's shoulder. "Ladies?"

Amanda straightened herself and looked back into Emily's eyes. "Well, someone needs to be in charge of *him*, at least."

"I will calm him down," Kiami insisted. "Since he won't answer the door, I am just going to go look in his window and see if he will let me in."

# 3

# Kiami - The Unique Youngling

Kiami wasn't sure what to make of Justin's behavior. They had returned to his house, as he had wished, and yet he still seemed to be brimming with hostility.

She hadn't missed the way he had stared resentfully at Amanda after they had arrived before proceeding to lock himself in his guest room. Had he insisted on returning just to have a safe place to throw a tantrum?

She didn't like it. There was more to his behavior than he had let on back at the castle, she was sure of it.

Stepping lightly around the outside of the house, she transformed and lifted her gray and silver wings in preparation for flight.

From her previous visits, she knew that only a few inches of wood jutted out below the bedroom windowpane. It would not be enough for her to easily grip.

Kiami glided by the window and then turned back to make a second pass. Justin sat on the edge of the bed, and by some small miracle, the window had been left wide open.

Although Kiami had her doubts that she could make it through the circular hole, she proceeded to move in a large loop around the house and then flew straight at the opening.

At the last moment, she adjusted her wings, folding them in around her, and moved to dive through. She closed her eyes as she felt herself propel forward and hoped she would make it.

Her hurried approach was far from graceful as she reopened her eyes and attempted to land in her usual way; instead, she skidded forward across the floor and came to an abrupt, painful stop as she collided with the side of a toppled dresser.

Kiami righted herself and shook from head to talon before casting her eyes on Justin. A box she recognized rested on his lap. He had been riffling through the contents, much as she had on her previous visit.

Startled at her intrusion, his face had turned a bright red. "Who do you think you are?" he seethed through clenched teeth.

She forced herself to return to human form, wishing she could have quietly observed him instead of rushing in the way she had.

She thought she saw tears glistening on his cheeks as he let out a light gasp and wiped at his face. She knew she was correct.

"A friend." Kiami looked around. "This, everything that has happened, is a lot to take on... even for those of us that have been raised with magic our whole lives." She sat beside him cautiously. "I am sorry that I startled you by flying in here like that."

Justin's shoulders sank as if the fight had drained from him all at once. "It's not what you expect. You hear stories of jinn and other magical creatures going off and defeating some monster, thing, some evil or other, and it always seems so... exciting and well, easy."

"That's because when they retell the stories, they leave out the really tough parts, and the teller usually isn't emotionally attached." Kiami grasped for his hand. "I think it's always hard. If it wasn't, then there wouldn't be any evil left."

"I know what Emily said back in the castle is true. I have just never felt like an outcast here, in this village before." He looked up into her eyes. "I just needed to feel closer to my parents. I..." He gulped and wiped at his damp cheeks with the back of his hand.

"Miss them," she finished. "Trust me. I get it. When my mother died, I felt so alone, and then my other guardian left me. There is still a hole there. I think there always will be."

He shook his head. "I wanted to feel closer to them because I needed to try to remember."

"What do you mean?"

"I was there when they got in their accident. Just a kid. I was so shaken up, I wouldn't even talk to anyone for days. And by then, they couldn't trust my memory." Justin paused, attempting to wipe away more tears. "Did I cause the accident? I will never really be sure. When they found us, it was just me and my mom. Jinn disappear after death. They turn to dust like they never existed at all. They couldn't tell if I had inadvertently caused it because my jinn abilities were manifesting in unpredictable ways, and I guess I was kind of a brat... How could I live with the thought? So, I became a joker to try to cover it up, my fear..."

Kiami wrapped her arm around his shoulders. She understood. After all, hadn't she been blamed for her own mother's death? And it almost felt like it was true, even now. "Do you want to tell me what you remember about the day it happened?"

Justin closed his eyes and breathed out a sigh of despair. "Can you keep it to yourself?"

She nodded but momentarily shifted her gaze to the floor before looking back up into his pleading eyes. She didn't like the idea of keeping the others in the dark about what was bothering him, but if it was the only way he would share his story, she would do her best.

"It was my birthday. I had been alive another human year, which for a jinni would be a blink of an eye, but my mom enjoyed celebrating the event, and since I seemed to mature at a more human rate than that of a true youngling, I did too."

He opened his eyes and looked up into hers. "My dad wasn't big on acknowledging human customs. He liked to focus more on jinni accomplishments, which for me felt so few and far between...

"That is why I decided not to go with him when he went into town to run errands. I chose to stay behind and help her prepare. We had barely mixed the cake batter before he returned.

"As he tore us from our fun, my biggest concern was when we would get back to bake the cake."

"That's understandable. You were young." Kiami patted his hand.

Justin shook his head and brushed his hair back from his face. "They were visibly upset with one another, which was something I didn't see too often. I didn't want to make it worse."

"What do you mean?"

He cast his eyes to the floor. "I felt a strange tingling sensation shortly after my dad had buckled me into the car, but I didn't understand it until I reached out for my mom in the front seat. My fingers and palm seemed to shimmer; I could see right through them. I tried to conceal my excitement as it bubbled up within me.

"My dad had talked to me about many of the things jinn children could do, but because I wasn't like the other younglings, I only had a vague idea of what could be happening to me. After all, my dad told me over and over that I am unique. So when my mom looked back at me from the driver's seat, I shoved my transparent hand under my leg to hide the condition and wiped the smirk from my face. Once she looked ahead again and I heard the engine roar to life, I knew she hadn't seen.

"I remember being so disappointed when I pulled my hand back out from beneath me, because it had returned to its usual state of flesh and bone...

"I stared at the back of my father's head as they talked, wondering if I should tell. I knew I was supposed to say something every time, but he seemed worried enough. I hadn't missed the way he wrung his hands together in his lap or the creases in his forehead that seemed to grow deeper with every passing second.

"Before that moment, if asked, I would have insisted my father was not afraid of anything. That's when I finally stopped worrying about myself and tried to figure out what was going on.

"But it was too late. I had been so distracted. I had heard only snips and pieces of their murmured conversation, and their words meant little to me.

"I knew only a few things for sure. Something had happened while my father was in town running errands, and he had raced home to collect us because he was trying to keep the jinn in town safe.

"When I felt the tingling sensation again, I tried to ignore it, to push it away. But instead, the sensation grew, prickling all over my body. I looked down, and the seatbelt strapped across my chest had moved through me. And then it happened so fast." He leaned in closer to Kiami's ear and whispered. "My dad yelled from the front seat. I will never forget his words and the strangled sound in his voice. He said we had endangered them all. We should have told them the whole truth from the beginning."

Kiami could tell repeating the words bothered him. It was clear to her that he thought his father was blaming him for causing the danger, and she nodded to indicate that she understood.

"I looked up at him to see him looking back at me. Our eyes locked, and I tried to force a scream out. It felt like my voice propelled from my mouth, but the noise never hit my ears."

He paused, his eyes darting around the room as he rubbed at the goosebumps that had formed on his arms. "The car seemed to fall away beneath me, just as it seemed my voice did, then there was a sudden blinding flash of light, followed by complete darkness. Like someone had flicked on a bulb in a pitch-black room and turned it right back off."

He stared back at Kiami, his eyes wide saucers. She was still mulling over her response to such a tragic event, and when she failed to respond, he looked away. "Even after, with the aid and guidance of other jinn, it was a long time before I had the courage to acknowledge that I had any jinn abilities. I was convinced that it was me, that I was the thing my father was afraid of."

Justin's hair had fallen back into his face, and Kiami pushed it away with her free hand. "A child's memory can be untrustworthy. It is easy for them to slip into different worlds and block things out when faced with something terrible. This can in turn cause fears that should never have existed."

"You sound like Gemma."

A playful smile spread across Kiami's lips. "She must be wise then."

He rubbed at the back of his neck. "The glimpses of the memory started after I got in a car accident with Emily. It happened a short time before you arrived. And everything that has happened since has compounded it, making me feel a bit overwhelmed."

He swallowed hard, and Kiami tried to keep her face blank as the memory of the incident swirled in her head.

Justin didn't know it, but she had been there, and she was pretty sure that she had been the one to cause the catastrophe. Warmth crept up her neck as he continued, threatening to stain her cheeks red, and she knew if she didn't tell him, the guilt would eat her alive.

"It wasn't a big deal or anything, not really. It had been dark, raining. Something had caused me to swerve, and I lost control."

Her mouth felt dry as she opened it to interrupt. "I was there. It was me; I think..."

She had broken his train of thought, and he stared back at her with a confused look.

"I stayed to make sure that you were both safe. I'm sorry. It's kind of embarrassing."

"Are you saying that you were there the whole time?"

Her heart sank. She could only hope that he would understand. "As you know, Aden brought me back to the human realm to find Emily."

"To spy. Yeah, you told us."

Kiami sighed and nodded. "After Aden left me alone on the road, a frightening creature appeared, and I panicked." She questioned if she needed to explain further about the beautiful, dangerous one-horned species, but decided against it. She needed to focus on the facts.

"You see, it wasn't the first time I had seen the animal, and I believed that it had somehow followed us from the Arcane realm. Anyway, long story short, I changed into owl form to escape, and I am almost certain that you were swerving to miss the animal as it attempted to chase me."

"That seems like quite a coincidence. I mean, it chased you right into the person that you were looking for?"

"Trust me, I know. I thought about it a lot after it happened."

"And you don't think Amanda could have been responsible?"

Kiami shook her head. "No. I don't."

Her response seemed to make him uncomfortable, and he fidgeted and looked away. "Listen, Justin, I don't think that it's really Amanda that you have a problem with, but rather what is happening to everything around you ever since she edged herself into your life by sending me here, and if that's the case, you should have a problem with me too."

"You and she are not the same."

Kiami didn't agree, but it wasn't the time to push the subject. She could see that she was making him upset again by the way he turned away to his avert his eyes so that they could no longer meet hers.

They sat in silence for several minutes before Justin turned back to face her, and Kiami picked up the box, trying to change the subject. "Did you get this stuff from Gemma?"

His shoulders slumped. "No. Those are things that were left here for me after the accident with my parents, before I moved into town. Cherry stayed here with me for a while. I don't know how she ever managed to convince me to leave. I felt like I was abandoning them... but eventually, she did. I left that behind. By then I wanted to forget. They told me it would all be here waiting for me when I returned."

"I know it's hard to think about. Try to be happy you got to know them." She shifted through the pile of letters and pictures as if it was her first time. They looked alike, she could see it now, him, his father, and his mother.

She had never looked anything like her guardian, Jacqueline, or her mother, Rhiannon. She just looked like herself.

She set the box back down haphazardly, causing the contents to shift sideways and reveal a small box wrapped in shiny paper. She recalled noticing it when she had gone through the box before, and this time, it stirred up a few of her own painful memories.

The worst was the last encounter with Jacqueline, and as it flashed in her head, she moved her hand to her chest where her beautiful necklace had once hung.

Even though the stone had brought her joy for only a mere few hours before she had lost it, she yearned to have it back. She felt like she needed it. She sighed. The possibility of ever finding it seemed slim.

She closed her eyes for a moment and imagined that she still had the gemstone fastened around her neck. She had been pleasantly surprised by the gift, a seemingly transparent stone, until she had held it up into the light, revealing a fantastic silvery blue that shimmered from within in such a way that she could only compare it to a sparkling star in the night sky. She had fastened it into a necklace right after she received the gem.

Kiami let her hand fall onto her lap and opened her eyes. Even if she had lost it in the scuffle on the beach, it would have long since been swept out by the tide or buried deep in the sand along the shoreline.

Justin squeezed her hand. "Now it's my turn to ask, are you okay, Kiami?"

"Yeah, sorry, you just had me thinking about my home." She pointed to the unopened package. "Why didn't you open that?"

Justin shrugged. "I had probably had enough surprises for one year."

He curled one side of his mouth up into a half smile. "I don't even remember where it came from." He jumped up from his seat and headed for the toppled dresser. When he reached it, he bent at his knees to heft it back into the proper position.

"Could I help you with that?"

He shook his head. "How about you tell me a little about your home while I clean up my mess?"

"My home..." She thought for a moment as she watched him pick up the box of memories beside her and toss it on top of the dresser, the unwanted gift still inside.

Although Kiami always tried to maintain an optimistic approach to her circumstances, opening that unexpected present had given her one of the few truly joyful moments she had experienced since her mother's death.

Her stomach knotted, and she couldn't help but wonder if she would have been better off not opening her last present as well.

It had been, after all, what happened after she had fastened the gem around her neck and wandered happily onto the beach that had caused Jacqueline to leave her.

Would she be willing to trade those few happy moments if it meant that Jacqueline would still be in her life?

Justin cleared his throat as he reached for some scattered papers.

Kiami sat up straighter. Calling up an image of her childhood home brought a genuine smile back to her face. "I lived in a house that was built up on a cliff's edge. It was quiet and peaceful and yet not. The ever-present sound of the waves crashing against the shore, the call of the sea birds as they flew over the beach below. It was - it is perfect." She corrected herself. How could she describe the comfort that the cool caress of the breeze brought her, or the taste of salty air...

"Sounds like a lonely place."

She sat up straighter, taken a little aback. "Well, it wasn't. People visited the beach all the time." She smiled sweetly at him, wondering if in his frustration he had purposefully made the comment to try to make her upset, or if perhaps she had just been around too much negativity lately.

"But not you. Isn't that why you left?"

She tilted her head. He was more like Amanda than he would like to admit. "I didn't leave until Erol came for me." She paused, thinking of Jacqueline and then of the way the wisps had frightened her when they appeared. "But I wasn't alone. The wisps had come."

He looked back at her, his eyes full of curiosity, and cocked his brow. "I'm sorry if I upset you. Your house sounds lovely."

"It's fine, nothing, you just reminded me of something that I left behind at my house before I joined Amanda in the Arcane realm."

Justin sat back down beside her. "Did the wisps show you something? What was it?"

It was true that Amanda and Emily had both said they had helped them. Kiami scrunched her nose as it dawned on her that the wisps may have wanted her to take the book from beneath the bed at her home. "This is going to sound strange. I think it was a journal. I never really had a chance to look inside. I had forgotten about it."

"Why don't you go back and get it?"

Kiami shook her head. "It would be selfish of me to go now. We can only solve one dilemma at a time. Maybe in a day or two we could go back and look for it."

"We? As in all of us?" For a brief moment, his eyes had sparkled with what had appeared to be excitement, but as he spoke now, they seemed to cloud back over with disappointment.

She shrugged, not wanting to make promises she wasn't sure she could keep. "Maybe. It could give us all more time to clear our heads. If ocean air is good for anything at all, it's that."

"Can we go now? I mean me and you?" he pleaded.

"Don't you want to get some rest?"

Justin only shook his head.

She had the sudden urge to be in the open, to feel the earth beneath her feet and breathe in the outside air. "Why don't we go take a walk instead?"

Justin sank lower. "I guess."

"Good." She nodded, pleasantly surprised that she had persuaded him so easily. "We will have a refreshing walk, then when we come back, you will rest. We can't be sure what tomorrow will bring."

# 4

# Amanda - Enigma

"What do you think they are doing up there?" Amanda tapped her fingers on the mantle above the fireplace. Paranoia had been creeping in ever since she had divulged to Kiami that she had witnessed the incident on the beach.

It had been before URD attacked the castle in the Arcane realm, and Amanda was sure now that things had settled down, it would only be a matter of time before Kiami put two and two together, linking her to Jacqueline's disappearance.

Emily shrugged. "Talking would be my guess."

"Yeah, but about what?" Amanda didn't want Kiami to look at her the way Justin did.

For the first time, Amanda wished a vision would overtake her so that she could listen in. Of course, the chance that it would be Kiami's mind she would invade, even if she had a vision, would be small.

"We will all go to town soon. Don't you think we need a breather? We have barely rested."

Amanda plopped down on the couch and sighed. "No, I don't want a breather. I don't want to stay in the human realm any longer than I have to."

Emily raised a hand to quiet her. "The jinn wanted us to go to town together."

Justin cleared his throat from the staircase behind them. "We were supposed to help Aden steer her in the right direction. No one said that we all had to stay together at all times, Em."

Amanda noticed Emily's cheeks turn a light pink. "Separating right now seems like a very bad idea. Don't you agree that we are safer together?"

He shrugged and made a slow descent. "I think we should stay in pairs, sure."

"You and Kiami want to wait here?" Emily questioned.

"Not exactly," Kiami spoke up. "We were talking about going for a wa-"

Justin shook his head, cutting her off midsentence as he exclaimed, "We were thinking of making a trip to her home."

Kiami shot him an annoyed look. "Justin! That is not what we decided."

Amanda's smile widened. "So this is his idea?" Even though she didn't really want Justin to accompany them to town, she did want to know more about the little expedition and why they were planning it.

Kiami turned to face Justin, eying him. "Not exactly. We were talking about doing that in a day or two. Maybe." She crossed her arms over her chest and moved her eyes between Emily and Amanda. "If you must know, my mom had a journal, and I was discussing the possibility of going to get it when this was all over. Justin asked if we could go now." She glanced back at him again. "And I thought he agreed. I offered a walk outside in the fresh air as an alternative."

"At least tell them why we think the book is important, Kiami," he whined.

"It was something that the wisps had shown me, or at least now it does seem that way, after having talked to you and Emily about the things they did for you. It is possible that it could be helpful."

His eyes glazed in disappointment, and she looked down. "But I do think he needs to get away..."

"Are you sure that's what he needs?" Amanda wanted to ruffle Kiami's feathers, just to see if anything else had been discussed. As it stood, she wasn't worried about them going to her home by the sea to look for the journal. Jacqueline hadn't been kidnapped until after her mother's death, so it was safe to assume that no information about Amanda was hidden within the pages of the book she was looking for.

Amanda turned to Emily and whispered into her ear, "I think you should let them go. Kiami will keep him safe from himself."

She saw annoyance flash across Emily's face as she took a step backward.

Justin intervened, "We didn't have to ask."

Kiami paled, no doubt remembering how she had called her actions selfish before, when she had been in the dungeon. "I don't think Emily wants us to separate right now, and I can't say I blame her."

Satisfied that Kiami had barely even thought about her experience on the beach, Amanda spoke up, directing her comments at Emily. "Nobody is going to get any rest here. Can't you feel the tension in this place? Let them go."

"Why does my opinion matter then?" Emily turned back to Amanda and eyed her as she addressed Kiami and Justin. "I am not in charge. Just go, you don't need my permission."

# 5

# Emily - Angst

Emily glared at Amanda after the pair left. "Now what? I don't suppose you just want to sit here and wait for them?"

A stern look was etched upon Amanda's face as she responded in a flat tone, "You want to be mad at me, get in line."

Emily squeezed her eyes shut for a moment in an attempt to keep the feelings of self-pity that welled up inside her from surfacing. She wanted to remain stern. "You could see the reluctance in Kiami's eyes. Don't deny it. Why did you pressure her to go with him when she clearly had reservations?"

"Can't you tell that he can't stand to be around me, Em? It makes this whole thing worse. So much worse."

"I don't know, Amanda. I am not convinced that this is all about him hating you personally. Remember what he said back at the castle: he feels betrayed by his jinn family."

"Oh, you know there has to be more to it than that. That's why we are going to go upstairs and have a look around."

"That wouldn't be right."

"Well then, what would you suggest? He certainly isn't going to open up to me."

Emily reached up and twisted one of her curls tightly around her finger before releasing it to spring back. "I am worried about him."

"See? That's precisely why you should be in charge, Em, and they both trust you."

Emily shook her head and rolled her eyes at the comment. "I guess it can't hurt to take a look." Irritated as she was with Amanda, she had to admit that she was right in one respect: Justin trusted her, and she hadn't been a good friend. She should have been up there with Kiami when they were talking.

Kiami and Justin had left the porthole open, and strong gusts of wind blew into the room, pulling pictures and letters up and out of an open box that sat on the dresser. Emily raced to gather them together as Amanda bounded forward, securely latching the window shut.

At a glance, the letters all appeared to be written to Justin from people his parents had known before their death.

Emily had been aware that his parents passed away; he had explained to her how he lived in the town with Cherry until she and Gemma agreed that he was old enough to come back here to stay by himself.

Emily stacked the items neatly and carried them back over to the open box. Gawking, she set them down on top of the dresser. The only thing that hadn't been blown out of the container was an unlabeled package. The box was wrapped in a familiar shiny paper. Emily's breath caught in her throat as she ran her hand over the bulge in her pocket.

The package looked identical to the one she had opened on her eleventh birthday. The one that had contained her stone. "It's not possible," she whispered.

She dug into her memory, trying to recall when exactly he had said his parents passed away. He had been just a kid like her when she received a very similar-looking gift. She chewed at her lip, wondering how old he had really been. She remembered that jinni do not age the same way humans do, and she had no way of knowing what rules would apply when you were only half jinn.

Amanda's hand darted out in front of her, and Emily grasped her forearm just as her fingers reached out to the metallic-looking wrapper.

She looked up to see an excited terror in Amanda's eyes.

"Don't." Her voice cracked as the memory of what happened to Toby when he had innocently grabbed her amethyst flooded her thoughts.

Amanda didn't move to pull her arm out of her grasp. Instead, she turned to look into Emily's eyes before letting it drop back down into the otherwise empty container. "Fine, but don't you want to know?"

Emily lifted her other hand and picked up the pages, placing them on top of the gift. "Don't I want to know what?"

"What's in the box, of course."

"If he wanted it open, he would have opened it." She could hear the twinge of fear in her voice, and she cleared her throat in an attempt to mask it.

"Maybe he is scared to open it, Emily. Maybe if we open it... At least tell me what bothers you about this box. I can see it all over your face."

"It gives me the creeps because it looks familiar. I know it's just my imagination. There are probably thousands of presents handed out that look like that one every day."

Amanda crossed her arms over her chest. "Okay, then open it."

Emily shook her head and backed up a step, still clinging to Amanda's arm. "I don't think I will."

# 6

# Amanda - Manipulation

As Emily released her arm, they moved toward the edge of the bed in unison.

This was going nowhere fast. Amanda had hoped she could get Emily to agree to peek in the box without revealing the truth about her visions.

Amanda had not received her stone in the same way, but she could not wave off the similarities between this package and the one that Emily had received with her amethyst inside. Surely if Justin's held the same type of gift, it would prove a plausible connection between the people in her visions, whom she had come to refer to as hosts, and herself.

The idea worried her a little.

If the package did in fact hold a similar gift, it would mean she would need to take Kiami to the tomb in an attempt to retrieve her lost gemstone.

She had witnessed Jacqueline tear the stone from Kiami's neck on the beach and then later saw her burying something in the tomb of lost things. She had thought it could have been Kiami's gemstone, but she hadn't had a reason or a way to verify that at the time.

Now, she needed to know.

It was evident to Amanda that Emily remembered her own package quite clearly. The fact was that she was being quite stubborn about the whole thing, and Amanda was running out of ideas to persuade her to open the box.

Amanda felt a twinge of guilt for pushing her as she looked up to see her worried expression, but it was short-lived. It would be for her own benefit, Amanda was sure she would see that in time once she realized and accepted that she should be the one to lead them. She stared hard at Emily for a moment.

A muscle in her jaw twitched as Emily questioned her. "Have you ever received a box like that one?"

Amanda mulled over her response for a bit before moving her mouth into a lopsided grin and saying, "I have seen someone open a box like that before. Would you care to guess what was inside?"

"No." Emily drew her lower lip between her teeth and nibbled it, her nervousness apparent. "I think we should go into town now after all."

With the change of subject, Amanda's smile slipped, and she wondered who had manipulated who here. "Without Justin and Kiami?" She raised her eyebrows. "What are you scared of? Not me, I hope?" This wasn't the outcome she had expected. It seemed as if the tables had been turned on her.

"I just don't want to be here anymore."

"Didn't you just argue earlier that we shouldn't be splitting up?" Perhaps she had pushed Emily too much. To conceal her own very real apprehension, she responded in a tone that she hoped sounded like sarcasm. "What if they decide to enact old deeds of revenge on me for being half demon-blooded? Are you going to be able to protect me without your friends?"

"That's not what I meant when I said we would be safer together, and you know it. You can trust the jinn in town."

"Emily, I can't trust anyone." She felt immediate regret for letting the words slip out, but it was too late, and it felt like the truth. "And maybe you shouldn't trust me either," she added. The damage was already done. "Perhaps they just wanted to lure me here for that exact purpose." Her mouth snapped shut and set in a hard line as she pressed her lips together.

"Revenge for what, exactly? You can't truly believe that they would want to harm you just because of your heritage. And didn't you say that you wanted to go to the village earlier?"

Amanda nodded, giving up on her attempt at getting Emily to open the box. Although something about going into town was making her uneasy, it was true that there could be valuable clues there. She knew it wasn't just her heritage that was giving her doubts, but also the things that Abaddon had told her when he manipulated her dreams.

"And if Kiami and Justin come back?"

"They will be gone for a while. You said so yourself, Kiami lived far from here by the sea. We can leave them a note."

# 7

# Kiami - Sandcastle

Kiami had noticed a significant shift in the atmospheric pressure before they left Justin's house. She didn't have to be in owl form to feel the difference in the air. Her senses were somewhat heightened even when she was in her human physique.

The shift meant that there was an approaching storm, and it felt like it was going to be a doozy. She had experienced changes like this often enough and out of curiosity had once read about how with the rise and fall of barometric pressure, owls could sense changes in weather.

The thing that seemed most off to her was the fact that when they landed, the air felt much the same here as it had at Justin's. In her experience, the weather rarely worked that way with places that were not close to each other geographically.

Now, as she stood unmoving, staring up at her childhood home, she wished she would have listened to those internal instincts given to her by her owl counterpart. Her arms dangled limply at her sides, and she breathed heavily.

Her home was not as she had left it. She could see empty patches where the shingles and siding were gone, as if they had been ripped away. Several windows seemed to be missing whole panes of glass. Yet stranger still was that no broken pieces of wood or jagged chunks of glass appeared to litter the unkempt ground around the property.

Justin made no sound as she felt his hand slide over hers and give it a light squeeze. At least she didn't have to go in alone. Wisps or not, to her, the house still felt like it was full of ghosts.

The skin prickled on her neck and arms, but it wasn't the haunting memories or the condition of the house. To her, it seemed as if the air hummed with electricity.

Justin tugged her forward.

"Wait."

"Kiami, let's go in. Once we are inside, it won't seem so, so…" He twirled his hand around in front of himself, indicating that he was searching for the right descriptive word.

She turned to face him. "Ominous?"

He nodded. "That's the one."

She took a hesitant step forward and looked into Justin's eyes. How could she expect him to forget his thoughts when she couldn't control her own? The familiar sound of the ocean waves lapping against the shore did little to slow her pounding heart. She inhaled the familiar scents deeply. Still, she couldn't calm herself. "You are absolutely right."

They began to approach the dark, empty house, slowly at first, but with each step, she gained momentum until she pulled Justin with her at a half jog.

Without even her to care for the property, it had fallen into a state of disrepair that she had never seen before or expected. It looked like ages had gone by since anyone had pushed those front doors open. A musty smell rose up from the home's foyer, and cobwebs riddled the walls.

Amanda had told her time moved differently in the other realms, but she hadn't been prepared for this. Something didn't seem right. How much time had passed since she traversed these halls?

The days that she had been in the Arcane realm after Amanda forced her to return there as a prisoner should have been negligible, even when coupled with the amount of time in which she had first grasped Aden's hand and accompanied him to that same castle as a guest.

Despite time moving more slowly there than in the human realm, it couldn't account for this. The house was in utter disarray after what could only have been a few weeks, two months at most.

She approached a tattered blanket that lay in the middle of the floor and lifted it with two fingers, holding it out at arm's length. She inspected it for a moment and then allowed it to fall back into a clump in the very spot from where she had lifted it.

What was more, to her, it looked like vandals had ransacked the house at some point. Items were displaced, shredded, and smashed. Cushions were gutted. The foam padding was torn. Many pieces of furniture lay overturned.

She wandered from room to room on the lower level, evaluating the damage. Somehow, a fair amount of sand had built up against many of the walls, as if it had been swept there by a broom or pushed there by a not so gentle gust of wind.

She returned to the foyer, where Justin waited. "Why is there sand all over? Have you noticed it? It is in every nook and cranny down here."

He didn't say a thing, just watched her reactions. She tried to shrug it off. She knew he had never been inside her home before and could offer no real insight.

Kiami approached the banister and sighed loudly as she laid a hand on top of the rail. She offered Justin a weak nod. "The book was upstairs."

A light hand landed on her shoulder. "I can go up alone if you tell me what to look for."

She closed her eyes and shook her head. "We go together. I am not sure what has happened here. But it's not *natural*." She stressed the last word to make her point.

"You mean this isn't how your house always looked?" he teased.

Kiami turned her face up at him, being sure to smile. She was glad he was joking again, but in all honesty, it didn't really seem that funny to her right now.

Despite what had happened to her since her mother's passing, she had loved her home, and these changes were hard for her to bear. She wondered if the damage could ever be reversed, and then scolded herself for thinking about it. There would be a time for worrying about things like that, and it wasn't now.

Usually the optimist, she forced her smile wider and then faced the front to traverse the staircase.

The steps creaked and groaned in an unfamiliar way as she placed her feet down, and she couldn't help but ask herself if the weight of her very thoughts was making her feel heavier. It was all so strange.

At the top of the stairs, the doors to the rooms seemed to be closed tightly all the way down the hall, and for a moment, she considered the possibility of the rooms being untouched by whatever the destructive force had been.

She shook the thought away as the breeze blew against her skin from a broken window farther down the hall.

For no real reason, she stood before each door, pushing them open one by one and then turning away from the mess within. Each time, she would move on to the next with a slow and calm approach, even though she knew she was just building the suspense within herself. With each swing of the door, she became more nervous, as if she was half expecting something sinister to leap out at her.

When she reached the bedroom where she had seen the journal, her hand hovered above the knob, and a chill ran down her spine.

Something else had changed as she passed down the corridor. Similar to what she had noticed outside, there was a hum in the air here too, as if it had followed them. Although she knew it wasn't plausible, it gave her the impression that the very walls were breathing.

Justin brushed her hand aside. "Allow me." He turned the knob and pushed the door open in one swift movement before she could protest.

She jumped back, startled, but as she followed him past the threshold of the room, she could see that there was nothing beyond the same battered, frayed, and ripped possessions they had encountered behind all the previous doors. She scolded herself.

The toppled shelves, torn from the walls, and the broken items scattered across the floor didn't hide some monster. She was just grieving for her once beautiful, now rather shabby house.

She forced a smile back onto her face before looking up at Justin and moving deeper into the room. Before she could comment on her own silliness, the floor seemed to shudder beneath her feet. It felt to Kiami like the house quivered with her thoughts as she continued through the bedroom, or what was left of it. She told herself it was her own imagination, a natural response to the sad sight before her.

The mirror was shattered, the drapery removed from the window and discarded on the floor. The dresser was toppled. Nothing much remained intact.

Justin cleared his throat breaking her concentration. "Where was this book, exactly, when you last saw it?" She pointed to the floor by the cracked and splintered frame of the four-poster bed.

Justin lifted the mattress and peered underneath. He shifted the ragged blanket and tossed aside the hole-riddled pillows. It reminded her of how she had lain there breathing in the familiar scents before she left for the castle. She doubted that the smell of her aunt still lingered on the dilapidated and moth-eaten rags.

"It's not here, is it?" she whispered as Justin returned to her side.

With her words, the house seemed to quiver again, but much more violently, and she crouched to the floor as Justin spoke. "What the..."

Her eyes went wide as she realized the movement she had sensed had not been her imagination after all. The walls seemed to shake and rattle all around them, and Kiami reached for Justin's arm.

The house tilted beneath them, and debris slid across the floor. The building seemed to rumble and groan in protest.

Even though they were sitting still, Kiami began to feel as if the world around her was spinning. She refused to release Justin from her grip as a wave of blinding dizziness assaulted her. The ocean sounds were drowned out by a whooshing noise. Colors seemed to run together, blurring objects in the room beyond recognition. For a moment, it felt as though she was hanging in thin air as reality shifted.

Just as suddenly, everything went silent. The swooshing and electric hum ceased. She couldn't hear the lapping ocean waves or the seagulls that were almost always present just outside. It was too quiet.

She didn't say anything to Justin as she pushed herself up off the floor and made a hurried approach to the window. The air there felt hot and dry. She leaned out, careful not to graze herself on the broken glass.

The ground outside looked a singed brown. The vast ocean was nowhere in sight. It had been replaced by a sea of endless sand dunes that stretched out ahead as far as she could see.

Justin sounded groggy, as if he had just woken from a nap. "What just happened?"

"I am not sure. I think maybe we moved with the house to a different realm. I want to go outside and look around."

Fear invaded his voice. "What if it happens again and we get stuck here?"

If she was right and the house had somehow jumped to a different realm, it would explain some of the damage. "How else can we see?"

Justin shook his head and folded his arms over his chest. "It seems like a bad idea to leave the house."

She couldn't argue with that. He was right.

"What if we don't have to leave the house?" Kiami said, thinking of the skylight she had used on occasion to go in and out.

He pushed his hair out of his face. "What do you mean?"

She waved to him to follow. "Up, we are going up."

As they neared the skylight, she changed into her owl form and wiggled through. From the roof she could see that the house really was surrounded by desert; in fact, to her, as she peered over the roof's edge, it looked to be halfway buried in the sand.

She wondered if you could even walk through the lower level. The bright sun felt hot on her feathered form as she waited for Justin to join her.

As she moved around the outer area of the roof, a reflection of light in the outlying area caught her eye, like the sun was gleaming off something. She could only assume it was a rooftop far away in the distance. She wanted Justin to witness this first-hand.

She turned around to start moving back to the skylight and was relieved that he had finally joined her on the roof.

His hand was planted on top of his head as he exclaimed, "Holy cow," as if he had been pushing his hair back from his eyes and stopped mid movement from shock at the sight before him.

Kiami moved back toward the edge, pointing with one of her talons.

"I don't see anything, Kiami."

She dropped her talon. She had forgotten she had above-average vision. Which meant if she was unable to get her eyes to focus on the buildings far off in the distance, he probably couldn't even see the twinkle that had caught her attention to begin with. Still, she wanted to explain what she seen.

Just as she thought of changing back into human form, a barrage of new sounds hit her exceptional ears. It sounded like faraway hoofbeats plodding through the sand, somewhere behind her, perhaps hidden from view by the rising dunes. Her heart skipped a beat when she heard the first neighing, although she was almost certain it was not a pack of unicorns. Time seemed to slow as seconds passed into minutes before she could make out pinpricks of movement in the distance. She realized that the riders must have been traveling around the sandy hills rather than trying to move over them.

Each horse carried a person on its back, and as they made their way closer to the house, they began to form a line shoulder to shoulder.

Among the sea of chestnut-colored mounts, one rider stood out. Unlike the others, the gray-haired man seemed smaller, less muscular, and he was not clad in the same white clothing as the men that surrounded him. Although he didn't really look like the others, Kiami got the sense that he was in charge. His silvery robes billowed behind him as they rode forward.

She changed back into human form, sure now that Justin would be able to see the approaching cavalry. In the short time it took her to transform, a dozen thoughts and questions crowded her mind.

She didn't know if the riders wanted to search her house or destroy it, and she wondered how many times this had happened before. It was possible, she thought, that they could be the very same intruders who had ransacked the place.

"Justin, do you think we should go out there?" She still didn't believe they should charge ahead into this unknown world, but she wanted to see if this new development had changed his opinion.

He shook his head. "We stay within the house."

"I agree."

"Good."

"But do you think they might have the book?" The more she thought about the journal, the more curious she became about the possible secrets written on the pages.

"I think the better question is how and why is the house moving between realms?"

"Yes, well, maybe if we describe this to Amanda, she can at least help us to figure out where we are. Then maybe we can return."

"I think we should worry about what's happening now. We don't know what their intentions are. We need to go inside and arm ourselves."

Kiami nodded, although she felt a bit embarrassed that she hadn't thought of that herself. "Of course." She quivered. "But Justin, what if the book says something about my abilities, and they are looking for me?"

Justin shrugged and shook his head. "Does that make a difference right now?"

Her shoulders sank and she lowered her chin. "Not really, no."

Justin moved through the skylight as she returned to owl form. He was already scavenging for weapons when she reentered. She hesitated at the thought of changing back again. She had never done it so many times without longer breaks in between, and she worried about the toll it would take if she needed to defend herself.

She stared after him as he rushed from room to room, piling broken items in the hallway, and she felt guilty that she wasn't helping.

They didn't know for sure that the riders knew about her or that they would mean them harm, but if the state of the ransacked house was any indication...

Her thoughts where interrupted by a startled squeal from Justin, and Kiami made up her mind. She couldn't be any real help to Justin inside of a house as an owl. She pushed at her magic, willing it to return her to human form.

Sure enough, the magic seemed to take longer than usual to respond. The delay reminded her of when she had been hurt at the castle and had attempted to transform. It wasn't until Emily had tried to heal her that things seemed to get any better.

As she made the slower metamorphosis, a light pain that she didn't normally feel during the quick process reverberated below the surface of her skin. It wasn't a debilitating pain, but it was notably uncomfortable.

Once the transformation was complete, Kiami began shifting through the pile of items. There weren't too many recognizable things that she would consider helpful in their current plight. She selected a portion of broken bedpost for her weapon and hurried down the hall to find Justin.

He was standing near her bedroom window, clutching a brass fireplace poker. She recognized it as being part of a set left in one of the guest rooms. She stepped up beside him to see what had startled him.

A black spider no bigger than her thumb was crushed on the floor in front of him. As his eyes locked onto hers, she had to stop herself from smirking.

His face seemed to morph from fear to anger and then to embarrassment before he spoke.

"It came out of nowhere. I... It just startled me. Please. Don't go telling the others about this."

She nodded as she glanced over his shoulder out the window.

The line of riders was now circling the perimeter of the house. One of the riders leaped down from their mount and began to approach the entrance. Kiami wrapped her hands around the makeshift wooden club in nervous preparation.

She gestured at the window with her weapon. "We have more important things to worry about."

She was so engrossed in the actions of the horsemen that she barely acknowledged the fact that the static hum had returned. It thrummed in her chest and head. "Justin," she whispered just as a low tremor pulsed beneath her feet, "do you feel that?"

His eyes became large saucers as he looked back at her and nodded. "Get down." As they both moved down onto the floor, she felt his arm wrap around her back. She let her weapon drop beside her. There was no point in holding it. The floor shuddered beneath them. The walls began to waver, and she closed her eyes in anticipation of the dizziness she had experienced with the last shift.

The house tilted, and she heard objects clatter as they rolled around.

The fearful horses began to whinny in protest. She heard cries from the men, but strain as she might, she could not make out their words; the language was unknown to her.

Soon their voices were drowned out and carried away with the sound of the hoofbeats as the horses began a hurried retreat. Her eyes watered as she squeezed them tighter.

She wondered if the man that had tried to enter managed to escape with the others. Then everything went quiet as her reality shifted. For a moment, it was if she was in both places at once as the smell of the sea and the house's rot mingled.

She didn't open her eyes or attempt to move until the sound of the waves crashing against the shore reached her ears. After a moment, she could taste the sea air in her mouth, and she looked up at her travel companion. "Justin, let's get out of here."

He looked back at her and nodded, a bewildered expression etched on his face. They made a hasty exit from the house, hand in hand, as if they were worried they might lose each other on the way out.

# 8

# Emily - Jinn Village

Oddly, the village seemed empty. Its deserted appearance sent a chill through Emily. The only time she had seen it look so vacant had been her birthday.

On that day, all the townspeople had waited, hidden in the diner, to surprise her and welcome her as one of their own. Even though she was not born from jinn heritage as they were, they offered her sanctuary there and explained about the secret powers they possessed.

She turned her head toward the diner, but it looked completely dark as she glared in its direction. It made her anxious to see the town this way, so uninhabited, and she found herself wondering if Amanda could have been right after all. Had her new family sent them to retrieve her only to lure her into a trap?

Emily maintained her smile and tried to mask her worry. She didn't want to give Amanda a reason to doubt the jinn any more than she already had. She was certainly on edge, Emily thought.

Amanda had been sure to bring her staff along, and now she hung on to it so tightly that her knuckles looked white.

Before she had crossed the border into the town, Amanda had questioned her about the magic fortification she had mentioned. Emily replayed the conversation in her head.

"You said it stops those that wish harm to the jinn from entering the town. You don't mean these jinn any harm, right?"

Amanda shook her head.

"Then there shouldn't be a problem. And if they didn't want you in here, they would be blocking your entrance."

"Maybe it's a trap."

"If it is a trap, I have your back. I promise." She had turned away from Amanda to move on, hoping that her statement exuded seriousness. But Amanda had continued to question her anyway.

"But you said yourself they are your new family."

Emily clenched her teeth, wondering if Amanda was somehow feeling her nervousness. "I can't win with you, can I, Amanda?" It had still taken more coaxing, "Remember back at the castle, I said they sent Aden with us because you would trust him. They can't speak about certain things... and they thought he could get past it. Do you really think they would have gone through all of this trouble just to harm you?"

"You would know better than me, I guess."

With that, Amanda had finally given in and moved forward.

The rest of the walk to the storefront was silent as they hurried along. Emily was too troubled by her thoughts to talk to Amanda, too busy pondering how she could help if it was a trap.

Just as they made it to the front of the bookstore, she wondered if Justin was having the same doubts. She was certain something like that could be playing a role in his behavioral changes.

The store looked like it always did, with its cluttered shelves and piles of books seemingly stacked around the floor at random.

She was relieved when Gemma appeared from behind one of the biggest stacks.

"Where is everyone?"

She opened her mouth in a wide smile as she pulled Emily into a hug. "I have missed you at the store."

"'I've missed you too," Emily said as she stepped back out of Gemma's grip.

"Anyway," Gemma added, "everyone is preparing to go to a safe place to wait the storm out. I suggest you all stay inside Justin's house for the night. It's going to be a big one. Didn't you see the sky?"

Emily nodded, realizing that Gemma was referring to the sky's strange coloring, which she had noticed earlier in the day. "But Kiami and Justin have already gone. They needed to retrieve something from her house."

Gemma raised her eyebrows and crossed her arms in front of her. "And

Aden?"

Emily shuffled her feet as Amanda answered, "He is not coming back." She moved closer to Gemma, wrinkling her forehead. "Why did you send them to summon me here?" She could hear irritation in her voice, and Emily flinched as Amanda waved a hand in her direction. "I have a feeling that you knew they would all be in serious danger in the Arcane realm."

Seeing her reaction now caused Emily to wonder if perhaps Amanda's comments and actions had planted the seed of mistrust that had been growing within her all day. Amanda was seeing red and not thinking straight. Emily's eyes widened as she glanced back and forth between them.

For a moment, it seemed as though anger flashed across Gemma's features, a shadow, but as Gemma took a step toward Amanda, the shadow seemed to clear. "They would have been in even more danger by not going to find you. We all would be."

Gemma reached a hand out toward Amanda, and Emily was surprised to see that she accepted it. "You will all need each other."

Emily reached out and grasped Amanda's free hand, waiting as they regarded one another. She felt as if they were having a silent conversation.

"So, Aden, he's not coming back at all, is he?"

"I fell short. I couldn't save him. In the end, it came down to another choice. I'm weak. We both know I don't belong here."

"You're not weak, Amanda; in fact, we worry the opposite is true. We know that without you, Erol would never have gained his freedom. You cared for him. You cared for them both."

Amanda said, "Everything inside me is dark and twisted."

"We are all outcasts here in one way or another."

"They are not like me."

"Of course. You are different. What good would it be if you were all the same?"

Amanda's voice lowered to a whisper. "I've been hiding so long, I can't find me anymore. Some days, I feel like I can barely breathe." Emily was a bit startled by the honesty of her statement.

"We all feel lost from time to time after having to step off the smooth path and into the harsh, dense jungle. We often stumble on a root or rock along the way. Sometimes we have to spend time with wild animals in the dark, but if you keep forging ahead, you will find the edge of the path again, and you will reemerge."

Emily squeezed her fingers, hoping that Gemma's words were as inspiring to Amanda as they were to herself. She was reluctant to bring it back up but felt she had to. "Now that Aden isn't here…"

Gemma cut her off mid-sentence. "His absence poses a new, different problem.

"So I have heard," Amanda said, shaking both her hands loose and stepping back.

"Let me have a crack at figuring it out with her," Emily said in an excited rush.

"Just be swift. Something's coming, besides the storm. We can feel it. There is strength in numbers. You feel it, don't you?" Gemma's brows furrowed.

Emily nodded; even though this time she wasn't sure what Gemma was referring to, she wanted to ease her mind.

"You had something else to tell me, didn't you, Amanda?"

Amanda shook her head, causing Gemma to raise her eyebrows and cast a knowing glance to Emily. "I will leave you to it, then." She placed a hand on Emily and Amanda's shoulders as she addressed them both. "It will take all that you are to get through this."

As Gemma left, closing the entrance door behind her, Emily turned to Amanda. "Are you okay?"

Amanda looked sick, her arm crossed over her abdomen as if her stomach was turning with the thoughts that reeled in her head. The color had drained from her face as she opened her mouth to speak. "Sometimes I wish I could feel things like you."

"We will never stop trying to reach you."

"What if I have nothing left to give?"

"Amanda?"

"It's Abaddon's lies. I feel sick just thinking about the things he said, the memory of his putrid smell, the way he looked, everything."

"Describe him to me. Maybe it will help."

Amanda raised an eyebrow. "I doubt that."

"Just try."

"He was a terrible creature. He was always grinning at me, showing off his grimy yellow pointed teeth. His skin had a dull gray sheen that exaggerated his bloodshot eyes and that tangled mass of green hair that puffed up from the top of his head."

"They weren't just dreams, were they?" Emily asked.

Amanda shook her head. "I thought they were at first. Something my mind had concocted because of the things I had seen. But when he invaded my sleep, his presence was so real, I could smell the foul odor of his breath. To hear him speak would send a chill down my spine. Then one day I made him angry and he left a mark on my flesh. Once I knew he was real, the things he was saying started to make sense."

"Is that what Gemma was talking about?"

"I couldn't tell her. I have been thinking about some things Abaddon said to me." She gulped. "You need to know, he mentioned that he couldn't manifest himself in town, but he also said that he had an anchor in the center. A place where he could spy on the jinn villagers. He knew when they had Errol; he said they had captured him. He told me details about the town."

"It was probably just a distraction so that you would keep reaching for the wrong puzzle piece. Let's forget about it for now. There are more important distractions down there."

Emily pointed to the familiar wooden door that led to the underbelly of the store. She wished Gemma could have gone down with her, if only to offer some sort of signal if she got something wrong or misrepresented an image.

As she pulled the door open, she realized it was much heavier than she had ever expected.

# 9

# Amanda - Lair

The bookstore was nothing special to Amanda, but her heart pounded anyway. It was the conversation with Gemma that caused it.

She moved down the sloping, winding passage, only giving a single nod as Emily pointed out that there was no noticeable source for the light in the tunnel. The magic that produced such illumination was no shocking surprise to her after the things she had learned while living in the Arcane realm.

She hadn't been joking when she said that the memories of Abaddon had made her feel nauseous. She paused as her stomach knotted, and steadied herself against the wall.

They weren't heading to a basement — it was the path to some sort of underground lair.

This path that led down to a room below the bookstore also rekindled memories of the time she had been trapped below the forest before she had been kidnapped by the sorcerer, Jacob.

"Weird, isn't it? You know, when they brought me down here, I had to wonder if I wasn't being transported to another place entirely."

Amanda scoffed, unimpressed, thinking of the strange places she had been since this whole thing started. She felt the corner of her mouth lift in a half smile as she thought, *This girl hasn't seen anything yet.*

She noticed Emily pinch her nose as she crossed through the rounded stone doorway that led into a larger room. She realized why, as the scent of incense and mothballs invaded her nostrils. She was surprised she didn't break out into a sneezing fit.

"This way." Emily moved in a circle, gesturing to the colorful paintings on the stone walls of the cave. "You are familiar with the myth of creation that the jinn pass on?"

Amanda pushed away thoughts of Jacqueline as she responded, "Yes."

Emily pointed to an image. "From what I remember, this seems to be the beginning. See the outline of the two forms here? I think those are the celestial beings from the story."

Amanda had read the myth in a book while she was being held against her will by Jacob and had heard it again from Jacqueline when she captured her. Although she hadn't taken Kiami's guardian or the book seriously, she remembered the story.

She looked at the dark image. Yellow dots exploded across the empty space, and sure enough, she could see the vague outline of two forms within it. She reached her hand out and touched the painting. Her words came out as a whisper, even though she didn't mean them to. "The myth of the planet Sumir."

"So you know the story?"

She lifted her hand and looked over her shoulder at Emily. "Yes."

"With the jinn physically unable to speak about it, they made these to try to preserve the history."

"But why go through so much trouble?"

Emily looked at her with a light but serious expression. "You would know, if you had ever bothered to learn, that the jinn always had a soft spot for humans. Maybe they knew deep down one day the truth would have to be discovered."

"Trying to decipher the truth from these paintings seems like an impossible task. Unless you're seeing something I'm not?" Amanda brightened the dimly lit wall with the glow of her staff and to recall the exact words of the myth.

*In the beginning, our universe was a great empty void. This void, it is said, contained space for endless worlds. One day, out of the void, emerged two powerful celestial beings, Eaki and Aya. They had traveled from another universe in search of a place where there was room for their godlike children to grow. They had brought with them the knowledge of creation and set about molding a simple world to live together in the center of the universe.*

*One by one, as their children were born, they raised them to adolescence. Knowing that at this age, their children would begin to become restless and crave a deeper purpose, they sent them out into this universe to create a single world of their own to cultivate and control. They were each given a limited number of enchanted supplies to use. That is how our sun, our moons, and each unique planet came into existence.*

She moved around the room, piecing the story together with each new image she studied.

*So it went until Aya gave birth to triplet daughters: Sophia, the firstborn, Akila, the middle daughter, and Mia, the youngest. The two younger siblings bickered constantly and fought for their parents' attention. As the girls neared adolescence, their competitive nature only grew worse.*

*Sophia overheard Eaki and Aya discussing her two younger sisters and was troubled to hear that they doubted the girls would be able to sustain their creations for long. When the time came, Eaki gave them each a chunk of enchanted clay, seeds, and some drops of his celestial blood. He then sent them into the universe to create their individual worlds.*

*Sophia followed her sisters, and watching them bicker and fight, she decided that they could not be trusted to fulfill their father's wishes. Determined to help them succeed and make her father proud, she persuaded them to combine the resources to create one larger, more diverse world together so they could share equally in the responsibilities.*

*Akila and Mia eagerly handed over the halves of their clay that were meant to be the basis for their three small worlds.*

*Sophia lumped the pieces of clay together and carefully started to shape the world. As she worked, the younger sisters teased and tormented one another. Sophia borrowed inspiration for many of her designs in this new world from stories her parents had told her of their favorite planet in the distant universe they had come from. She created a flat mass of land and surrounded it with water. She molded rivers, mountains, and valleys. When everything seemed to be balanced, she shook the remaining tiny flecks of clay from her hands, creating small stars in orbit around the world.*

*Satisfied that she had included everything required for obtaining harmony, she went to work molding a race of humans. Sophia carefully considered every little detail before applying the final touches and bringing them to life. To her, free will was the only real gift they needed to thrive.*

*Sophia was content with the intelligent beings that she created and enjoyed watching them learn and progress. Mia and Akila also watched the humans. Although the humans were quite intelligent, they appeared weak to Mia and Akila. The sisters decided they would each make a magical race and have a contest between them to decide which of the two could create the most powerful beings. Akila created the elemental spirits, the jinn, born of smokeless fire.*

*In response, Mia created beings with great arcane magic and taught them to hate the jinn and to pursue them relentlessly.*

*As the two races fought one another, Sophia's race of humans was often caught in the middle. Not having natural magic themselves, they were unable to put up an adequate defense. Sophia couldn't bear to see her humans so abused, so she jumped down onto the plate of land, splitting it into several pieces and spreading them apart across the great seas that she had created. Hoping to spare her human race from future devastation, she placed them all onto one of the masses of land.*

*Akila and Mia continued to pit their creations against one another, but* it became clear that the two species were somewhat equally matched. Still, craving victory, Akila used the last of her clay to create beings of pure light and energy. In response, Mia created demons of pure darkness, able to harness the shadows.

Again the sisters sent their creations on a path of destruction. By this time, all being intelligent and curious species, they had discovered various ways to travel the great seas. Once again, humans were thrust into a war they had no chance of surviving. Sophia scolded her sisters for being so careless as she watched her humans brought to the brink of extinction.

Still, the sisters ignored Sophia's plea to stop their ruthless campaign. The battles raged on until only two humans remained. Sophia's anger grew, and she was filled with rage at the destruction of the creations that she had worked so hard on. She ripped and shredded the very fabric of the world, tearing each species away from the others and separating them into five different planes, with the humans in the centermost realm. Once these changes were made, Sophia knew they could not be undone. Still disgusted with her sisters, she created two more planes; the realm of the goddess was set above all of the other planes. She forbade her sisters from joining her there.

Into the seventh plane, she threw her remaining ingredients at random. Sophia then ordered her sisters to live in that realm of chaos far below the other planes. Only then did her younger siblings stop bickering amongst themselves. Seeing what had befallen their world, the two younger sisters felt guilty and longed to earn back Sophia's favor.

Akila and Mia still had a few supplies remaining, seven drops of creator's blood and seven seeds from the sacred tree. Akila took the tree seeds and put them in each new plane that had been created, connecting them once again in secret locations that would allow passage from plane to plane.

"Emily, look at these stones here." Amanda pointed to an image as she thought of the next piece of the myth.

Mia created seven powerful gems to represent each of the planes and offered the stones to Sophia as penance. Sophia had missed her sisters and was *impressed by their gifts. She allowed them to remain with her in the realm of the goddess to help watch over the original five realms.*

She wondered if it was a coincidence that the black gem was shaped just like hers. "This black gem and the amethyst one." She recognized a third, oval-shaped gem. The artist had even attempted to make it look like it sparkled on the inside.

"Within every myth, there lies a speck of truth."

"What's that?"

"It's what she said to me when she brought me down here for the first time. Gemma said you must open your eyes to see it, even though you may not want to."

When Amanda had held Jacqueline captive, she had made a similar statement. *That can't be a coincidence*, Amanda thought as she moved ahead to another image.

"Those are supposed to be the gifts that the sisters created to make the barrier of the realms?"

"They said when the trees and gems were presented to the sister, the veil walls came into being."

"What if the trees are the connection, and the gems are the power source?"

Emily tapped at her chin, staring hard at the painting. As she dropped her hand back to her side, she said, "It feels like you're reaching."

"But they are even shaped similar to mine, and look at yours." She pointed at the image of the more elongated purple stone.

"We need more to go on than two gemstones that happen to look alike."

"Look hard at these gems. Which puzzle piece do you think is most important? What about Justin's box?"

"Coincidence. Justin can barely do the things other jinn do."

"Oh yeah? When did you realize you could heal things?" She watched as Emily bit into her lower lip and winced. She didn't mean to make her upset, but she felt like she had to push her a little more. "If you would have let me open it, we would know."

Emily shook her head and crossed her arms over her stomach. "So you got one of these boxes?"

"Not exactly. Erol gave me the black diamond."

"Then why do you feel so strongly about this? I just don't believe it. Even if that is the thing in the box, and if it happened to look like one of these here, that would only be three."

*Four*, Amanda thought as she reached up to touch the image in the picture that she was sure depicted Kiami's moonstone.

"Amanda, why do you feel so strongly about this?"

"I think I got mine first. I mean, I am guessing, but please bear with me. There was something he said to me. Everything has to come from somewhere. What if when he gave it to me, he set something into motion? Or maybe something was already in motion, and he helped move it along." She could see only disbelief registering in Emily's eyes. "I think Kiami has one, and I think I know where it is."

"If she had one, why wouldn't she say anything?"

"It was taken from her soon after she got it. She has forgotten or doesn't want to remember. It doesn't matter, because I remember, and I think I know where it is. The only catch is, she is the only person that can retrieve it—" Amanda suddenly stopped speaking.

Had she just implicated herself in Jacqueline's disappearance? Kiami already knew that she had seen her on the beach. It was discussed when she was captured. It would only be a matter of time, and surely she had just advanced it. But it was too late to take her words back now. "Em, isn't it too much of a coincidence that both of our gems seem to amplify our magic? After all you have seen and experienced, is what I am suggesting really so far-fetched?"

"So you saw Kiami with one of these gems?"

"Yes. I mean, I didn't know what I was looking at when it happened. It definitely added power to her magic." She pointed up at the moonstone in the painting. "It looked like this, only she wore it on a chain at her neck."

"Well, what do you think it means?"

She hoped Emily would assume that she had seen the necklace when Kiami came to stay with her at the castle, and she was relieved when she didn't pry more about the details of her knowledge.

"I really don't know for sure, Em. When do you think they will be getting back?

Emily looked taken back by the question, and Amanda wondered if she should have waited to reveal her ideas about the stones.

"Who, the jinn?"

"No, Kiami and Justin." Amanda raised an eyebrow. "Is there anything you're not telling me, Emily?"

Emily only shook her head in response, and Amanda couldn't help but question whether she was ready to find answers. It was true that it seemed like she wanted to help figure it out, but there was a big difference between saying something and acting on it. Maybe she had been wrong about Emily's leadership potential. "I think we should go see if they are back yet."

"Okay. I will bite, but I don't think we should tell them your theory, even if you are right about Kiami. We are still missing four more stones from the painting. Three, if Justin's box contains what you expect."

Amanda couldn't agree more. She shrugged to hide her enthusiasm. "What could it hurt? And like you said, it might be far-fetched, but I think it's something we should explore."

"I still think you're grasping at straws."

"Maybe, but we should find out."

Emily moved toward the door but stopped short.

"What is it?"

"It's just... It's probably nothing."

"Go on."

Emily pointed to a place on the wall. "I don't remember this being here before."

"Maybe you got distracted and just didn't notice it," Amanda suggested as she walked up to the image to get a closer look.

"Maybe, but I don't think so."

The image was a wide view of a landscape. Within it were two detailed gardens with a tree-lined footpath in between.

One was circular, with the bushes cut into the shapes of people, and the other was filled with small, flowering trees.

This second garden was enclosed on three sides by a smooth wall that appeared to be solid rock. There were several square carvings near the bottom edge. Each of them had a face chiseled into it and stone-carved hands that were protruding out just above the bottom of the square.

The ground below them, where the grass would have grown upward covering the carvings, had been paved in with small stones to form a semicircle.

The painting drew up the rest of the myth in Amanda's memory, and she recited it out loud as she studied it.

"As time went by, the creatures below in the seventh realm were all but forgotten. Left unchecked to mature and evolve on their own without the guidance of the goddesses, they became loathsome and villainous. Some of the beings blamed the humans' existence on the separation of their planes and were deeply resentful. Others missed the humans, especially the jinn, and passed the knowledge of what had happened down through the generations. Most humans forgot about magic altogether."

The image did seem brighter, and, she thought, a little more detailed than the others. She released a sigh. She was the daughter of an archaeologist, not an art aficionado. She really didn't feel that she could say beyond a shadow of doubt whether or not it was a new image, or even if it was created by the same person.

"Are you saying you think that's the Chaos realm?"

She shrugged. "Why not? It's the only part of the myth that doesn't have a painting."

"It doesn't seem chaotic to me."

"Em, looks can be deceiving."

# 10

# Kiami - Turbulence

It was a silent trip back to Justin's house as she clung to him. She had never traveled on the wind before, and she found it a turbulent bumpy ride compared with her own flying, even before the storm had interfered with their journey.

But she had decided it would be best if she didn't use her own magic to change back into owl form. She had thought she needed time to replenish her power. She regretted the decision even before they crash-landed in his yard.

Kiami had been frazzled, to say the least, as they fell to the ground. The rough winds and pelting rain had prevented them from making a perfect landing. It had been her second tumble in one day, and she was used to moving in a graceful manner most of the time.

When they entered the house, she was mentally exhausted. She spied a note on the counter, and relief washed over her when she realized that Emily and Amanda were not there. She didn't have it in her to explain what they had seen at her house. Not yet, anyway. She needed some time to mull it all over. "Here Justin, they left a note on the countertop." Kiami waved the paper back and forth. "It says they went to town."

Justin grabbed the note from her hand. "Figures." He barely glanced at it before he tossed it back down. "The moment we have something important to tell them."

It was clear to Kiami that he was already back in his sour mood, if it had ever really lifted to begin with. "Justin, I need time to digest what happened. I think you should take time too."

Justin glared at her. "Fine."

Before she could respond, something nuzzled against the back of her leg, and Justin threw his hands up in the air. "The whole planet is against me."

Kiami was more than a bit overjoyed to see Fizzle, and she ignored the way Justin stormed out of the room.

She looked down at the little beast with joy in her eyes; he was covered in some weird gelatinous goop.

Fizzle, this strange fuzzy creature, had first shown up when she was agonizing over whether or not she should reveal her human form to Emily and Justin. After she got over her initial fear of the animal, she had found his companionship to be comforting, and he had been popping in and out of her life ever since.

"What did you get into?" she asked, smiling. Her hands made a squishing noise as she picked him up. *Ew*, she thought.

"You're lucky you're so cute," she said matter-of-factly as she looked into his small, round eyes.

She called to Justin in the other room. "I'm going to take this guy upstairs and give him a bath."

He yelled back, "Whatever."

She smiled wider. "He will get over it, Fizzle. You are exactly who I needed to see."

Upstairs, she closed the bathroom door and placed him in the porcelain tub before engaging the plug and turning on the tap. As she reached for the bottle of shampoo, he jumped over the side and darted to the far wall.

"Fizzle!" she scolded. "Get back here!" He looked knowingly at her from across the room, wagging his stubby tail. His mouth was open, his tongue hanging over the edge as if he was grinning at her.

Kiami tried to scowl as Fizzle danced in front of the door, hopping on his stubby legs.

"Bath first." She wagged a finger at him in disapproval. He jumped at the closed door, and she could hear his claws as they hit the wooden surface of the floor in the hall.

She hadn't planned for him teleporting through the door. She hoped that Justin wouldn't hear the noise and come up the stairs. She cracked the door open and looked down the hall in each direction. "Fizzle, get back in here now!"

He sat still and let out a low, playful growl, as if he was waiting for her to come at him. She walked slowly toward him, but he darted between her legs and down the hall just as she got close enough to bend down and scoop him up.

He zigged and zagged from one wall to the other, enjoying the game of chase, and then vanished into thin air.

Kiami threw her arms up and stomped back into the bathroom. She hoped the wet, damp creature wasn't trying to dry himself on the furniture, as she had seen dogs do.

The sound of running water close by reminded her that she hadn't turned off the tap. She rushed back into the bathroom to see water spilling over the side of the tub.

She carefully reached over to shut it off before grabbing every towel and washcloth in sight as she worked to sop up the mess.

Just as she finished, she looked up to see Fizzle grinning at her from inside the warm, filled tub. She rolled her eyes and smirked at him in amusement. "What am I going to do with you?"

She hurried to soap him and scrub him as best she could before he could change his mind or tried to lick her.

As she released the plug, she glanced at the towels heaped on the floor.

"What a mess." She bent down to collect the driest-looking towel from the heap of wet cloth and proceeded to dry him with it. As she sat him down on the floor, he tried to slop a wet kiss on her face. "None of that now." She smiled down at him. "You always show up at just the right time, do you know that?"

# 11

## Emily - Weather Patterns

Gemma had been right. The rain began beating down before they made it back to the cover of Justin's home. It wasn't a refreshing rain, but a harsh one.

The wind sighed and the boughs moaned as they thrashed back at the pelting raindrops that surrounded the treetops.

Despite the downpour, the sky remained vivid, filled with a coruscating kaleidoscope of colors.

Thoroughly soaked from head to toe, her wet shoes squeaked across the floor as they came in from the rain. Emily was glad to see that Kiami and Justin had returned while she and Amanda were in the village.

Justin had been anxiously awaiting her arrival, and he jumped at the pair as soon as they entered, blurting out strange stories before they could even say hello.

It seemed that when they had arrived at Kiami's house, they were shocked to find it in a rather dilapidated state. As much as she wanted to break away and put on dry clothes, there was nothing to do but sit down and listen to what he had to say.

Justin told them about searching the rooms, then being moved, thrust, and torn from the human realm and planted in a harsh desert of unrelenting sun.

It was Amanda that first interrupted the tale, asking if they had seen any buildings.

Kiami must have heard the commotion, because she came into the kitchen, swearing that she had in fact thought there were buildings in the distance, though rather far away from where they had landed.

The events that followed their initial arrival seemed just as eerie to Emily.

Kiami had explained they were so bewildered by the change in scenery: they went up to the roof to get a better look at the land that surrounded the house, only to see a curious group of local riders or perhaps pillagers had set out for the home as soon as it had appeared.

From what the pair said, it seemed possible this was not the first time Kiami's house had appeared there, and it would help explain the weather-worn, damaged look it had taken on. In fact, to Emily, it also sounded plausible that the riders had been in the house before and were waiting for the chance to return.

When they finished the story, Emily couldn't help but feel that their explanation was a bit hurried. She wanted to hear more details, but she also wanted to get changed out of the wet clothes that clung to her.

Amanda tapped her nails impatiently on the table, and when Emily looked up at her, she raised one eyebrow expectantly. She had the feeling that Amanda wanted to take a break as much as she did, but she was trying to get her to say it. She glanced over at Kiami and watched her chew at the tip of one of her nails. It was evident that despite her usually calm demeanor, she was still a bit worn by the experience.

She felt a pointed boot kick to her calf, and she jumped up from the table and turned toward Amanda to see sly smile spread across her face. She bent down and rubbed at her calf. "Could we take a fifteen-minute recess?"

After Emily put on dry clothes, she made her way back to the kitchen table. She wasn't surprised to see that Justin had not moved from his spot. "You got any of that cocoa?" she asked as she slid into one of the chairs.

"Yeah sure." He stood up and cocked his head to the side. "You guys didn't say anything about your trip to town. Was everything all right there?"

Emily shrugged; she wasn't sure what to say about Amanda's theory. She still thought the whole idea was a bit of a stretch. She decided it would be best not to say anything for now. "We only saw Gemma. She said everyone was preparing for the storm."

"I'm not surprised. Do you hear that wind? It sounds like it could rip the roof off the house."

"So this is normal weather here?"

He set a steaming mug of cocoa down in front of her and shook his head. "Not that I remember."

Justin set a second hot cup in front of the chair across from her and sat down. "At least not this bad."

His answer worried Emily. "Do you think the townspeople are in real danger from the storm?"

Justin shook his head. "Gemma told you they were preparing by going to a safe place. I am sure they can take care of themselves."

Emily was a little taken aback by how callous he sounded regarding his family at that moment. It was obvious to her that he still harbored a grudge over the fact that they had kept things from him because he was only half jinn.

Kiami walked into the room with Fizzle running circles around her feet. She moved carefully forward, trying not to trip over him. "This guy." Her eyes smiled down at the critter as she shook her head. "This is the longest he has stuck around."

Justin took a sip from his cup and then stared down into it as he spoke. "I am sorry if I have seemed a little snappy."

He lifted his eyes to Emily, and she returned a cautious smile.

Kiami moved into the seat beside him and patted him on the shoulder. "It's okay."

Fizzle surprised Emily when he jumped up into her lap. Her grin grew as she spoke. "I was wondering when we were going to see the little dragon slayer again."

She patted the creature gently. He had been responsible for at least some of the good fortune they had been dealt during the encounter with URD. Possibly even saving Justin and Kiami's lives, he had distracted and poisoned the monster's minions, temporarily incapacitating them. She would be forever grateful to this little ball of fur.

Amanda appeared from around the corner. "Dragon slayer?"

"I was just being funny." Emily looked over her shoulder at her. "The first time I met this fellow, he grabbed one right out of the air in front of me with his tongue and then slurped it up."

Emily followed with her eyes as Amanda took a seat at the table. "But where were you when this happened?"

"Well, right here, actually. In the woods, over there, anyway." She pointed at the window, indicating the surrounding woodland.

"Curious. Are you familiar with those flying lizards, Justin?" Amanda asked, turning her face to him.

"First time I ever saw anything like them," he murmured.

"Well, as far as I know, dragons only live in the Emerald Mountains, which is the realm of the jinn."

Justin peered back down into his cup as if ashamed. "I don't know a lot about the Emerald Mountains."

Emily heard him shuffling his feet under the table. She could tell that he was bothered by the fact that Amanda seemed to know more about the jinn realm than he did.

Amanda shrugged as if it were no big deal. "I went there once; it seemed to be deserted." There was a distinct calm in her voice that suggested to Emily she was trying to be soothing, at least in her own way.

As Justin looked up and flashed a quick smile in Amanda's direction, Emily couldn't help but think that the trip had been good for him after all, even if it was short and full of surprises. He seemed to be trying harder; they both did.

"Anyway," Amanda added, turning back to face Emily, "both these events seem to reinforce what I was thinking back at the castle."

"Which was?" Emily prodded. "You never fully explained that theory." She stressed the word *that*, hoping Amanda would get the hint not to bring up the idea she came up with under the bookstore. "You mentioned the disappearing waterfall and..."

"No." Amanda shook her head. "That was only part of it. Remember what I said about that icy tundra me and you experienced? I thought we had been pulled into a different realm?"

She nodded. "I remember."

Amanda flipped her hands open and splayed them on the table in front of her. "I am pretty sure that what Kiami and Justin described is another realm I have been to."

Justin pushed himself back against his chair. "So you think the realms or the barrier that makes up the realms is failing?"

Amanda nodded. "But as usual, it just opens up more question such as how are we expected to help? Do the jinn think that we can fix it, and why?"

Justin shook his head. "There doesn't seem like there's enough proof to me."

Emily watched as Amanda muttered, closing her eyes and pulling her hands under the table. "Great. Another cynical member in this group. Look, I can't tell you why they are failing. I am still looking for a connection."

Emily glanced between them. She had been a little startled by Justin's response. This theory of Amanda's made sense to her. At least, a lot more sense than what she had suggested about all of them having mythical stones.

"Kiami, what do you think about it?" she asked.

Kiami pulled her fingers away from her mouth, exposing her mangled nails as she looked back at Emily. "It didn't really surprise me when Amanda said that the dragons come from the Emerald Mountains. Remember how alien the forest looked that day? Plants I have never seen in my life were growing everywhere. If she is sure that me and Justin traveled to a different realm, then I think her theory is feasible."

Justin crossed his arms over his chest. "And how can we know where we went for sure?"

Amanda opened her eyes and returned her hands to the table. They looked red to Emily, as if she had been squeezing them tight while they had been hidden from view.

"When you were in the desert, did anything stick out to you about the riders?"

Kiami answered, "Well, all of them seemed pretty muscular, and they were wearing white uniforms." She glanced over at Justin before continuing. "Except one. He looked older, thinner. He wore a long silver robe. I think he was in charge."

Amanda uttered a single word: "Bloise."

Kiami crinkled her forehead. "The wizard?"

Amanda nodded. "The one I told you about before."

"Do you think he took the journal?"

"I wouldn't put it past him. Maybe we should pay him a visit."

Emily leaned forward against the table so fast that Fizzle let out a yip and jumped from her lap. "We can't go out in this storm."

Amanda sat back in her seat. "Well, I agree with you on that, Emily."

Kiami gave a quick nod. "It doesn't seem natural. I mean, it felt like a normal storm at first, but now it feels different somehow. I can't explain it."

Emily could hear the sarcasm creeping into Justin's voice, and she winced as he spoke. "So what are you saying? That it's some kind of magic storm?"

Kiami jerked her head in his direction but maintained the calmness in her voice. "I'm just saying that I have never felt anything like it before." She turned to look directly at Emily as she asked, "What would you call it?"

## 12

## Emily - Stormwich

Emily halted the ensuing argument by insisting that they were all just hungry. They should be, at least, she thought. She couldn't even remember the last time she had sat down to a real meal, and yet she didn't want to eat. Her stomach felt knotted.

It seemed that Amanda wasn't the only one looking for her to take the lead. She wondered why all of a sudden everyone else wanted someone to be in charge. She looked at the food she had gathered on the counter. Maybe it was all in her head. Maybe they just expected her to be more assertive.

While she was stalling the preparation of food, the storm had seemed to kick up a few notches. The wind had gotten louder, and she no longer heard just rain battering the house, but solid objects seemed to be hitting up against it every few minutes.

She called Justin back into the kitchen to draw attention to the loud thudding. She thought that he looked a little annoyed at her interruption. She supposed she should have expected such a reaction and tried to wave it off. She had been the one to tell them to leave the kitchen in the first place. "Aren't you worried about that noise?"

"No, and you shouldn't be either, Em. I'm sure it's just fallen branches or other debris being blown against the house. It's solid construction. I promise, even if every shingle gets ripped off, we will be safe."

He glanced down at the food-covered counter and shook his head at her. "What are you making, besides a mess?"

She bit her bottom lip. "Sandwiches?"

"Thanks, but I will pass."

"Are you worried about the village now?"

"Nope."

"Well, I am." It was a half-truth. She knew they would do everything in their power to keep each other safe, but she had never seen a storm like this.

He shook his head. "Was there anything else you needed?"

"I guess not," she answered weakly. She had the sudden urge to tell him about Amanda's theories, in order to get his opinion, but squashed the idea down.

After he strolled back out of the kitchen, Emily looked at the bread, bewildered. What was she thinking? No one wanted a dumb sandwich, not when a magic storm outside sounded like it was ripping Sumir to pieces.

She wondered if the barrier was equipped to somehow protect the town from natural or magical disasters. She didn't care how cool Justin played it. He would never want his family to come to harm.

A loud thwack came from behind her. She turned to see a small frog squashed against the glass, stuck where it was. She swore it stared right into her eyes for a moment before it started slowly sliding down the pane. Was it raining frogs now? She couldn't tear her eyes away until it disappeared behind the windowsill, leaving only a trail of slime where it had moved down the glass.

She thought about opening the door to see if frogs really were falling from the sky, but instead she made her way back to the counter. She stared at the ingredients for a moment, wondering how she had become so intertwined in this, almost smushed together like a sandwich.

Her mind conjured up an image of the town surrounding her, holding her inside while some force tried to eat away at the crust. She could picture the large, grinning mouth that Amanda had described to her from her dreams, chomping down on her and all the people within it.

She pushed the image away.

The thought of loading the bread with meat and cheese made her knotted stomach turn. She put the supplies away and grabbed a few apples instead.

She tossed one to Fizzle as she entered the sitting room. He seemed happy enough as he gobbled it up. *Apparently*, Emily thought, *he is an omnivore.*

She carried the remaining apples over to the others and handed them out. "I decided a light snack would be best." She was surprised that they had all been sitting in silence.

"Fine by me," Justin said as he held the apple up to his face, as if examining it for contaminants.

When she sat on the sofa, Fizzle crawled onto her lap and laid back down. "He hasn't teleported at all since he's been here, Kiami?"

"Only when I gave him a bath, and he didn't go far."

"Do you think it's weird that he is sticking around?"

"Maybe he doesn't like the storm either."

"Maybe," she agreed. "Amanda, could you tell me more about Bloise?"

"There isn't a lot to say. I met the old wizard long ago before I knew about my true heritage. He was crude, to say the least."

"Did he say much about the power he borrowed? You said it was similar to mine."

"He said that it came straight from the goddesses and that it was something new. He didn't say much more, but to me it seemed like he talked about the goddesses in such a way that it made me think he knew a lot about them." A shadow seemed to cross Amanda's face. "If we do travel to see Bloise, I want you to be careful what you say around him." She shifted her gaze around the room. "All of you."

The lights flickered on and off a few times, startling Emily. She heard the sound of breaking glass upstairs just as the wind let out another fierce roar and the house went dark.

Earlier in the day, the sun had remained bright, even with the storm raging. She hadn't noticed when its brightness had begun to drain away. She moved to the window as the others scrambled to light candles.

Apart from the rain falling within her direct line of sight, the only thing visible was that strange moving patchwork quilt of color, although now the once vivid shading was much softer in appearance. Beyond that, she couldn't even make out the edges of the clouds.

Emily moved to an empty spot on the couch and plopped down. Someone had brought a few blankets into the room, and she pulled one over herself, clutching it to her chest as she listened to the wind and rain beating against the house.

The candles flickered about the room, casting eerie shadows on the walls as Justin moved to light the fire. "The window shattered in my bedroom. I covered it the best I could, but I'm not sure how well it's going to hold. We could all sleep down here on the floor, unless you three want to take the guest room?"

Before they could discuss sleeping arrangements further, Kiami reached up and covered her ears. "What is that?" she cried.

Emily looked at her as she wilted in her seat, bewildered by her actions. But before she could ask, a sudden ear-splitting howl echoed through the walls from somewhere outside in the distance, and then another. The sounds seemed freakishly high-pitched to her, as if the wolves themselves were screaming for mercy. It made the hair stand up on the back of her neck.

She knew that Kiami had noticed them first because of her sensitive hearing, which meant whatever was making the noise was getting closer and moving fast. "Do you think that it's another creature like URD or Abaddon?"

Amanda shook her head. "I don't think so — listen."

Emily concentrated on the sound. As the howls grew louder, they sounded like they were coming from all directions.

"It sounds like a whole pack of wolves," she said weakly as she shrank down into the cushions.

Although the window didn't light up, what sounded like the booming crash of a lightning strike came down around the house. When several of the creatures yipped and whined in response, the noise sounded like it was right outside the walls until they faded away.

As silence filled their ears, she pondered what had frightened the animals. Several minutes passed before Emily realized that the wind and rain had stopped. She had been so preoccupied by the howling that she wasn't sure how much time had passed since. She wondered why no one spoke as she shivered from beneath the blanket, unwilling to break the silence herself.

A hurried knock on the door ended the noiselessness, and Emily let out a strangled gasp. "See, who would be out in this unless its someone looking for us?"

Although he didn't move to answer the door right away, Justin was the only one that didn't appear apprehensive to Emily as she looked back and forth between the others.

It was Amanda that pushed herself up to run to the door, just as Emily heard it swing open, banging hard as it hit the wall.

Kiami stood quickly and followed, prompting Emily to get up and move along with them. She couldn't leave them to defend the house on their own.

As she joined them at the door, Justin followed behind.

A cloaked form stood in the entrance. It wasn't huge. Emily wouldn't even have described him as large, but as he stared into the room, the reflection of the lit candles burned in his black eyes as if he was staring through them. Emily remained frozen, staring back in his direction.

He raised one side of his mouth into a half-grin while the other side stayed limp and flat. His dark eyes rolled up into the back of his head, and he collapsed in a heap just inside the door frame.

Emily moved first, her magic suddenly pulling her forward toward the creature. She reached out one hand to push back his hood and caressed the wet, muddy, matted hair on the scalp of the fallen intruder.

But it wasn't him that her power was screaming at her to help. She felt nothing when she touched him. She righted herself and stepped over him to get past the entrance. In her hurry, she felt her shoe graze his stomach as she moved.

There was someone else just outside of the garage. The figure pushed himself up from the ground and hobbled forward. She didn't hesitate as she hurried to his side, reaching for his arm just as he lost his footing and fell back into a hunched sitting position. She squatted down to kneel beside him and was relieved to see that Amanda had followed her outside, staff in hand.

She could hear Justin and Kiami talking from the doorway, where the first visitor had collapsed, but the fuzzy sound in her ears made it impossible for her to understand their conversation.

Emily knew that there was no need to explain what she had to do when Amanda mimicked her position on the other side of the fallen visitor and nodded. She placed her hands against him and allowed the pushing wave of magic to wash over him.

As the static in her ears abated, she could hear Kiami scolding Fizzle when he growled and barked continually from inside.

Amanda wrapped one of the visitor's limp arms around her shoulder. "Let's get him upright and inside."

When she lifted, Emily grasped his other side with both hands to help support him. He was heavy, and she wondered how Amanda had managed to hoist him with one arm while still maintaining a grip on her staff with her free hand.

He lifted his face, turning it toward her. His voice sounded weak as he whispered, "Please help me."

"I have done what I can." She let out a grunt as he went limp in their arms.

Fizzle darted out of the doorway, running through the garage, right past them, still growling and snarling as they worked to carry the second visitor inside.

Emily sounded out of breath as she spoke. "He must have been really badly hurt. What do you think is wrong with Fizzle?"

"I. Don't. Know." Amanda paused after each word with the strain of the weight she was carrying. "Maybe. He. Didn't. Like. That. Guy."

Emily bit into her lower lip and felt warm blood fill her mouth. She hadn't meant to chomp so hard, but as she chewed, Amanda had stepped forward, jerking her and the visitor sideways, causing her teeth to sink into her flesh.

Justin stood blocking the door as they approached.

"Let us pass," Emily groaned.

"He could be anyone."

"So could he," she said, nodding toward the kitchen.

"Well, he is already inside." He crossed his arms over his chest. "He is still passed out. If he tries something funny, I can handle him."

"You heard what was going on outside. None of us knows what they were doing or if there were running from something," she argued.

"We. Can't. Just. Leave. Him. Out. Here."

Emily furrowed her brown and frowned. "That's it! Move!"

Justin backed up, and as they pushed past Emily said, "Do you think we can make it to the guest room?"

"Just. Keep. Moving."

"You stay where you are until we come back," Emily said, addressing

Justin.

After they made their slow ascent to the guest room, she waited for Amanda to recover. She felt a little guilty for allowing her to take the brunt of his weight.

Amanda breathed out, "I don't like this at all," as she propped her staff next to the door.

The visitor hadn't moved when they laid him in the bed and pulled a cover over him. "He must have been hurt pretty bad," Emily offered, thinking of how slow Kiami's recovery had been when Amanda hit her with her shadow magic back at the castle. "Should we leave him alone?"

Amanda lifted her eyebrows and crinkled her nose. "I don't think we need to worry about this one. Let's get back downstairs."

Emily was shocked to see that Amanda's whole disposition had changed by the time they made it back to the kitchen.

When they had rounded the corner to find the other visitor sitting at the table with Justin, she had dropped her arms to her sides and stared at the guest in obvious disgust.

She whispered, "Is everything okay, Amanda?"

"Just great," she breathed back.

Justin looked up at them then with a smirk plastered on his face. "Good to see that you both made it back down here safely."

Emily said sternly, "Like Amanda said, we couldn't just leave him out there."

Justin scratched his chin. "Yeah, yeah. My question is why did you put him in my guest room?"

The visitor broke in with a raspy voice that scratched at her eardrums like sandpaper on wood. "Where is everyone else?"

Justin glanced at him, still smirking. "Kiami went out to see if she could get Fizzle, that little animal, to come back in." He turned his gaze back on Emily. "Even after she let him out, he just kept running around the house, growling."

Emily glanced up at the closed door and then over at the visitor before addressing Justin. "That's odd. He was so calm through the whole storm. I wonder what's going on with that critter."

The stranger spoke again. "Shouldn't there be more of you?"

Emily raised her eyebrows at him, wondering why he didn't have the decency to introduce himself. "What the heck are you talking about?" she said, thinking, *and who the heck taught you manners?*

Amanda sneered at him. "Perhaps you bumped your head?"

Justin leaned forward on the tabletop and offered, "Our guest here was explaining to me that he was lost in the storm."

Emily thought she heard Amanda whisper, "Lies," just as Justin opened his mouth to speak again. "Amanda, Emily, you should join us. He was just going to explain to me how he ended up here."

Amanda placed her hands on her hips and stared daggers back at them. "I am more interested in hearing the other one's version of events."

She spun around on her heels to face Emily. "There are always two sides to a story. I will be upstairs with our wounded guest. I am eager for him to awaken." With that said, she stomped out of the room.

Emily gaped at her as she disappeared around the corner, not sure what that was all about. The only thing that was clear to her was that

Amanda didn't like him at all.

# 13

# Amanda - Aeron

Her muscles felt stiff as she stood and stretched. The visitor in the guest room hadn't stirred all night, and Amanda had fallen asleep sitting up on the floor with her back leaning against the wall. As she woke, she found herself curled into a ball with her knees pressed to her chest. Her staff lay beside her; she hadn't dared to leave it behind as she and Emily carried the wounded visitor upstairs, and she had regretted not having it with her when she had gone back down to the kitchen with Emily.

The sky had returned to its natural state, and the room was lit up with bright sunrays that streamed in through the small window.

She wasn't sure how best to deal with the situation. She had a feeling that the visitor downstairs was not to be trusted, but she couldn't just act on the feeling; she needed a way to prove it to the others and try to keep her secrets safe at the same time.

She hadn't missed how Emily had bypassed the hurt intruder as he lay on the floor, marching straight for the person outside. It was obvious to Amanda that her magic had been calling for her to help one over the other, and she didn't think that Fizzle's behavior was a coincidence either. Those things alone wouldn't be enough to prove it to the others, though. Especially Justin, she thought. For some reason, he had taken a shine to the visitor that had barged into the house uninvited, and yet he seemed disinterested and irritated by this one.

Although they had never met, she recognized the visitor on the bed as one of the hosts from her visions. She knew his name was Etzion, and when she had been thrust behind his eyes the first time, he had seemed like an average young man. That is, until she had witnessed him teleport, not from realm to realm, but from place to place in a matter of seconds. He had simply called up an image of the location that he wanted to be in, and the next thing she knew, he had moved from his home to school in not more than a blink of time, and all the while she was still there looking through his eyes.

He was one of them, she knew it.

Lines of worry appeared to wrinkle Etzion's forehead as she stood over his sleeping form, and she frowned. He had always been unmarred in her vision and had seemed to be content, even carefree, when he had been her host.

The pillow under his head was smudged with dirt. Deep scratches that had scabbed over were etched into the skin down one side of his face, and a large bump remained on his forehead.

Since Emily had attempted to heal him, she couldn't be sure of what had been inflicted upon him the previous night and what could have been present beforehand. Like Kiami, he must have been on the brink of death, or Emily's magic would have revived him much more.

The other visitor was a stranger to her. She was leery of him, but there was nothing she could do except try to play it cool.

As she descended the staircase and rounded the corner, she could overhear him talking in the kitchen, and she wondered if he and Justin had been up all night.

She stood still, listening for a few minutes just out of view as he rambled on in his raspy voice. His declarations sounded like bragging to her. But that didn't prove he was lying about the wolf-like creatures he claimed attacked him and Etzion.

Amanda propped her staff up against the wall and stood tall, ready to join the conversation.

"They had been following us for some time before they pounced, snarling and hissing. They were out for blood. I barely managed to save him."

When she rounded the entranceway into the kitchen where Emily, Justin, Kiami, and the visitor sat around the table, she could see that they were eating a light breakfast of fruit and toasted bread. A cup of cocoa rested in front of each of them. Steam still rose from the tops of the mugs, and she could smell the sweet chocolate aroma.

She cut him off as he opened his mouth to continue. "You didn't save anyone."

He looked up at her, gawking. "I didn't?"

"No, Emily healed him."

With her words, she saw that Emily's cheeks turned a light pink, and she lowered her face to the tabletop.

The stranger had been leaning back in his seat with his shoe-clad feet resting on the table, and now he slid his feet off the surface and straightened his chair. He looked around the table. "Those creatures came from the Chaos realm. I know it."

"And how on Sumir would you be privy to that information?" Amanda challenged.

Emily spoke up, "Amanda, it's like the dragons."

"So, you have witnessed what's happening? First-hand?" he questioned.

She could see a wide grin pasted on his smug face as he glanced up at her, adding, "I was wondering how all this is affecting the Emerald Mountains and the jinn that live there."

She sat down in an empty chair and shrugged. "There's not much there. The village of jinn was abandoned long ago."

Aeron was tall and muscular, but pale. To her, he appeared to be in his late teens. She looked over at him. "It is Aeron, right?" She had heard Justin say his name when she was still outside of the kitchen listening to them.

When Amanda would travel to excavations with her father, they would talk about the folktales of the people in the area. Often, they would end up comparing similarities in the stories to those that they had heard in other places. Although at the time she hadn't thought it noteworthy, names and their meaning would always come up during these discussions.

She had begun to believe names were important ever since she met Erol, but she doubted that it would make any difference to the others.

The name Aeron was a familiar one. If she remembered correctly, that name often had gruesome meanings like carnage and slaughter.

He grunted, "Yeah." Then he cocked an eyebrow at her. "So, you have visited there? A lovely place. Or so I've heard."

He stared into her eyes, giving her a look that caused her to think he knew there was more to the story than she was saying. "There have been rumors... and I wonder if you would have any idea what has become of the great and wise guardian that they say watched over the realm after the initial disbanding of the jinn."

Amanda set her mouth in a straight line and leaned in. "Rumors? I am more interested in facts. Such as the fact that the things you are saying are not common knowledge among the people in the human realm. So, where exactly are you getting your information from?"

Justin interrupted in a boisterous voice. "It sounds to me like we can finally get some answers."

"It sure *seems* that way," Amanda said, stressing the word *seem* as she sat back in her seat. She wasn't the least bit put off by Aeron's remarks. A good spy, a convincing imposter would need facts to back up his claims. He knew about what she had done to the guardian, probably even how she had disposed of him.

The newcomer continued to stare at her with his dark eyes, as if he expected a response to what he had asked before Justin interrupted. She decided it was best to ignore Aeron's inquiry, and she skootched her chair in closer to the table, turning toward Kiami. "Did you find Fizzle outside?"

Kiami nodded and averted her eyes down at her plate. Amanda could tell the way the creature was acting bothered her.

She had heard the way Kiami had yelled at him... it was unlike her. Kiami's hands were flat on the table, and Amanda reached over to give them a comforting squeeze.

Kiami squeezed back and then tucked her hands under the table as Amanda drew her own away. "He won't come in. Won't even let me pick him up. He's sitting just outside of the garage, the last I looked. Like he is standing guard."

"Don't you think that's odd?"

Kiami gave a halfhearted shrug with one of her shoulders. "I am not sure what to think."

Emily pointed at Aeron. "Did his friend wake up?"

Amanda shook her head. "He talks in his sleep, though," she lied, hoping to get a rise out of Aeron. She couldn't shake the feeling deep down that told her they weren't friends. "His name is Etzion."

Aeron blustered, "I could have told you that. If you had asked me, Em."

Amanda seethed at the use of Emily's nickname like he was a friend and not just some random untrustworthy creature.

As she looked over at Justin and their eyes met, he was quick to avert his, and the idea crossed her mind that she was thinking of Aeron in the same way Justin thought of her. She shifted her gaze as she assured herself that it was not the same thing.

Emily shrugged. "It didn't come up. You have hardly stopped talking about your own heroics since we sat down here."

Amanda smirked at the remark. Maybe Emily didn't buy his act either.

Justin broke his silence. "We should be discussing Bloise, and..."

Perhaps, Amanda guessed, he felt obligated to sound like he was in charge. She wasn't sure, but she wished he would shut up.

"What? Who is Bloise?" Aeron asked, turning to him.

Kiami had remained quiet for the most part until now. Something had seemed to quell her normal optimism, whether it was the state of her childhood home, or Fizzle's behavior, or perhaps the combination of both, Amanda couldn't be sure. "We need to meet him. He has something of mine that I need to retrieve." Hopefulness squeaked through her daze.

"He is a wizard Amanda has dealt with in the past. We are just trying to work it all out ourselves. This craziness with the things coming through the realms," Justin continued.

Aeron said, "We shouldn't; it sounds dangerous."

Even though she knew she was failing at keeping her cool, Amanda spoke up again. "Since when are you part of *we*?"

"Since I explained to them about the nature of our journey. We have been searching for others like us since I found him. You can't think three human girls and a half jinni can solve this on their own."

"First off, I am only half human, and well, I am not like most girls, am I?" She glanced between Kiami and Emily. "I can assure you that these three are not helpless either."

Justin sat up straighter, with obvious delight at being included.

"That's what I am afraid of," Aeron said.

"What is that supposed to mean?" Amanda couldn't keep the sound of spite from her words any longer, and it came out almost like a snarl.

"I simply mean it could be a trap. He took the item to draw you into him, to draw all of us in."

Amanda blanched as the memory of her first visit to see Bloise flashed through her mind. It was what she had overheard him say about her blood in particular that bothered her.

"What have you told Aeron so far?" She addressed everyone else in the room.

Emily cleared her throat and fidgeted in her seat. Amanda had noticed a growing look of discomfort on her face since she had joined them. "Nothing, really. I should have woken you earlier, sorry."

Kiami broke into the chatter. "He didn't ask much. He already seems to know a lot."

Amanda was cautious to pry further — not that she wasn't curious. She just didn't want to divulge information he didn't already know about.

She looked at the trio of familiar faces, expecting them to understand that she preferred them to keep things to themselves. "I am still more interested in hearing Etzion's version of events."

In response, he reached into his cloak, pulling out a small pouch and tossing it on the table.

Justin stretched forward, grabbing at the pouch and dumping it out in front of himself, revealing a light blue gemstone. He lifted it up to his face for inspection.

"This reminds me of Emily and Amanda's gems."

*He's good*, she thought. *He has props and everything.*

"Nice observation," Aeron remarked.

Amanda scolded herself, wondering how she could have dismissed seeing the familiar stone before. She knew it was Etzion's gem, but to explain it in a way that they would believe, she would have to tell them about her visions. She shifted uncomfortably in her seat. Even with the new understanding sinking in, she could not risk giving up the information in front of Aeron when it was clear that he didn't know about them.

She wondered if Emily would notice the similarities to the blue one in the painting. Amanda glanced at her, but it seemed that Emily was preoccupied. Her face was scrunched up and contorted in pain.

Amanda had forgotten the discomfort Emily felt after healing someone. She needed to put a stopper in the conversation so that she could help Emily as she released compounding energy. It happened every time. It was as if in a very literal way she lifted the pain and hurt from their body and after a time, had to transfer it somewhere else.

She rolled her eyes in Aeron's direction. "I have had enough of this. Don't tell him anything until his *friend* wakes up and we can hear his side of the story."

Her outburst seemed to shock Kiami and Justin, and they gaped at her.

She stood up from the table and glared in his direction. "I think you are an imposter, and I think you should leave."

"Maybe *you* should." His smile grew wider as he moved closer to her. When he reached her side, he whispered, "All those secrets that you keep are going to catch up with you eventually."

She clenched her fists so tightly that she felt the nails begin to dig into the flesh on her palms as she struggled not to run from the room. But it was Emily who did so first, and Amanda cursed under her breath.

She needed help, now.

As Amanda turned to follow her, Aeron reached out, grasping her arm. "Let me give you some advice."

She looked back at him dumbfounded as he stared into her eyes.

"Justin has hinted to me about how you manipulate the girls and have caused him to question his own family's motives."

Justin's chair squeaked across the floor as he stood up and bellowed, "Hey! That's not what I said!"

Aaron's eyes stayed locked on her as he asked, "Didn't you, though? Maybe you didn't say it in so many words..."

She didn't bother to look over at Justin as he dropped back into his chair. She knew he would have a defeated and ashamed look on his face.

"Stay away from them," Aeron said, motioning toward Kiami and Justin before he released her arm and turned away, whirling his cape out behind him as he moved.

"I don't have time for this. Emily needs me." Amanda hurried out the door, hoping that Justin would heed her warning and not say too much else.

Amanda stopped suddenly, and Kiami almost collided with her as she spoke. "I can't believe he just said that to you. Don't listen to him. We need you."

"Shh, I'm not," she whispered. "But I can only deal with one thing at a time. If we don't help her, she is going to hurt herself."

Amanda was staring at Emily's glowing form. Her fists were clenched at her sides, and she could bet if she saw her face, her teeth would be gritted together painfully.

# 14

## Emily - Pressure

All Emily could feel was the tightness in her chest clawing to get out as she had burst from the house.

She had known the rebound was inevitable, but she had hoped to wait it out as long as possible. The throbbing had been building and slowly escalating through the night since she attempted to heal the fallen stranger. Now it pounded in her ears. Her chest felt tight from the heaviness.

As she hurried to get away from the others, it became hard to breathe. The aching in her chest spiked. Excruciating pain shot through her. She stopped in her tracks, clenching her fists, and felt her teeth grind together as she tried to hold it in.

She could barely hear Kiami and Amanda's muffled voices from behind her over the pounding of her own heart and the familiar static sound in her ears as she breathed in and out.

One of them said, "Emily, we can help you." But she was unable to determine if it was Amanda or Kiami speaking.

She whispered through her gritted teeth, "Get away. Someone will be hurt." She couldn't believe they had followed her. They had seen first-hand the repercussions of her healing. Why would they do that!

She wasn't sure what caused it to tug at her so soon, so strongly. Had she felt threatened by the conversation? Like when URD had attacked after she healed Kiami, or when the man in the hotel attacked after she had healed Felicity? The fact was she wasn't sure of all the rules. But she knew it would happen eventually, one way or another. Maybe it meant nothing. Perhaps it was uncontrollable.

"Emily."

She shook her head. "I can't stop it!" The words burst from her mouth.

"Let us attempt to help you."

Kiami said, "I think maybe you can try. Like you did after you healed Justin. Direct it somewhere. Maybe not a rock this time. Try a living thing."

She thought of how she had tested pushing it at the rock and ended up hitting Kiami instead. It had been an accident.

The owl had swooped down out of nowhere and frightened her. She hadn't known the bird was Kiami at the time. She hadn't even met her yet.

Kiami and Amanda stepped in front of her, each reaching for one of her hands.

"Please, Em. It's a hunch. I have been thinking about it ever since I was following you in the woods that day."

Emily refused to take hold of their outstretched hands but moved forward toward the tree line, each step more painful than the next.

Her breath caught in her chest; the damage from the storm was unbelievable. She looked up into the perfect blue sky. That was the only thing that remained familiar. The once spectacular forest looked less appealing than a garbage dump.

It was all wrong. The trees that had flourished with vines and fruits were now bare. Many had been ripped from the ground and lay overturned with their roots exposed.

She bent down and touched a blade of grass. It seemed to be the only living thing that had survived the onslaught. Emily stood back up, swallowing hard, and looked helplessly at the girls. She couldn't hold it back much longer. Her shirt clung to her skin with sweat.

The sound still rushed in her ears, but she could see Amanda's mouth moving as she heard, "How could the wind and rain do all this?"

She watched as Kiami put a finger to her lips. "Shh, do you hear that?" Emily followed as she moved forward into the desolation.

The bleating cry sounded almost human, and goosebumps had erupted on her arms as they found the source of the eerie noise.

A fawn had been pinned beneath one of the large, uprooted trees.

"It's dying, Emily. Put it out of its misery." That was Amanda, she thought.

Its eyes looked dull as she bent down closer and placed a hand on its chest. Its heart was barely beating. She hung her head, wishing she could save the animal. But that wasn't how her gift worked. Once she healed something, the damage she took on had to be released somewhere else.

"It is suffering, Em," Kiami assured her.

She choked out, "Back away."

She felt a wet tear roll down her cheek, and she closed her eyes before she gave in and released the harmful magic.

She felt it tear out of her and the tightness dissipate. When the waves of pressure stopped, she stood, turning in the direction of Justin's home, and bolted back out of the woods. On the edge of the forest, she collapsed to her knees and covered her face with her hands.

Kiami stood over her and gripped her shoulder, trying to comfort her as she whispered, "I couldn't look at it. I just couldn't."

"It's okay. It will be okay." Kiami sat beside her and wrapped an arm around her back.

Several minutes passed in silence before Amanda emerged from the woods and joined them in their spot on the lawn.

Emily dried her tears and looked back and forth between the two young women with admiration. "Thank you."

Amanda picked at the grass. "It was Kiami's idea."

Her face was clouded with worry, much as Kiami's had been all morning. Even in her distressed state, she had noticed that Kiami wasn't herself.

"What is wrong with the two of you?"

Amanda let out a doleful sigh, and Emily turned her face toward Kiami. "It is one thing to see her brooding, but it's not at all like you to act so depressed."

A look of pain flashed across Kiami's face at the accusation, and then she pushed herself up off the grass, bouncing on her heels. "You are right. I don't know what has come over me. We should be happy to have more help to solve this puzzle."

Amanda tilted her head up. "You trust that guy?"

"Well, he sounds pretty sure of himself," Kiami offered.

Emily chimed in, "I admit that I was a bit distracted, but I thought that sapphire looked convincing. Isn't that what you were looking for, Amanda?"

Emily heard Amanda let out an annoyed grunt, and she threw her hands into the air. "You are so confusing! I thought this was what you wanted, to prove your theory about the gems. Well, he has one."

"It's not his. He is nothing more than a well-informed imposter."

"Why would you think that?"

"Well, for one thing, Fizzle doesn't seem to want us near him. After the way he helped us against URD, I would say he has pretty good instincts for a little monster.

Kiami let out a relieved breath. "I didn't even think of that when I was scolding him."

"And the gem?"

"Didn't you see the way he had it wrapped in cloth? I bet he stole it from Etzion."

"Wait, so you trust Etzion, who you haven't even talked to yet? But you can't trust the jinn or Aeron?"

"The jinn are not a threat to me right now. He is."

Emily folded her arms over her chest. "You need to explain why we shouldn't take his help."

# 15

# Amanda - The Confession

Oh, of course the imposter was willing to help. Amanda rolled her eyes. She understood why they didn't want to believe her, but their foolishness could get them all killed.

She had tried to recall even the slightest glimpse of this dark stranger, but could not. It wasn't that she didn't want his story to be true, but she had learned not to trust long ago, and his story just didn't add up.

She had little choice but to offer them more information.

At least they were outside, where they could talk in relative privacy. Amanda glanced over her shoulder at the house but didn't see Justin or Aeron at the windows, and she doubted either of them could overhear her.

"You seem worried that they are listening. I can keep watch if it would help," Kiami offered.

"You should hear this too."

"If you haven't noticed, I have great hearing."

Emily nodded and made a shooing gesture with her hand, which brought a smirk to Amanda's face. *Maybe she is ready to take on a leading role, after all. She just doesn't know it yet.*

She cleared her throat. "It's how I came up with the gem theory. Do you remember what I said when you took me below the bookstore to see the paintings, and you said I was reaching, but that blue sapphire matches the one in the picture, and so does Kiami's moonstone." She reached toward her in a friendly gesture, but Emily backed away warily.

They stood there eying one another for a moment, and Amanda's smirk faded.

"Go on." Emily motioned to her to begin.

"I should have told you from the start, but I didn't understand then. I still don't." Emily eyed her suspiciously. "I have visions. I have had them since before I defeated Jacob; they assailed me, frightened me. I wanted to try to figure out how we were connected, and I think the stones are part of what connects us, maybe even what causes me to have the visions."

Emily said nothing, but her hand reached into her pocket, and Amanda was hurt momentarily by the mistrust that showed on her face, the pain in her eyes. She was guarding herself against an attack, and Amanda wondered if after this Emily would lose what little faith she had in her when she explained.

"You were the person I saw open the package like the one Justin has tucked away."

"What?" Emily looked back at her, disbelief written on her features, and she placed her hands on her hips.

"I know you are skeptical. Even that I am not making this any better by holding back information. Just listen; something's not right." She looked at the ground as Emily tried to gaze into her eyes.

If the eyes were the windows to the soul, she didn't want Emily sneaking a peek of hers. She felt dirty. Her soul was tarnished with the things she had done, was still willing to do. She felt undignified.

"I saw you as a girl. You were having a party. I saw your mom's reaction, and I was a witness to your pain."

Emily folded her arms in front of her stubbornly. "And you left me there?"

"I didn't know who you were or how to find you, and then I hadn't had a new vision of you for years." Amanda felt as if she was going to burst into tears.

"Where is this going?"

"You have all hosted my visions, Kiami, Justin, Etzion..."

Emily interrupted, "So you spied on us?"

"No, it's not like that. I can't control them, and I still don't know what they mean." Amanda suddenly felt the hair rise on the back of her neck, and she scanned her surroundings. "Let's move a little farther from the house..."

"No," Emily retorted. "I'm not falling for any tricks. I want to make sure they can hear me scream if necessary."

"Emily, please," Amanda begged. "Just over there a bit, closer to Kiami." She stepped forward and was pleased to see Emily followed.

They stopped at the outer edge, not far from where Kiami had perched herself above.

"Get to the point, Amanda. You should have told us before. What are you threatening me with?"

"No, no, Emily, I'm warning you."

Emily turned away from her. Amanda touched her shoulder and felt her shudder in response. "Please, Em. Try to believe me, just this once."

"So, what are you saying?"

"The point is, Emily, that I have tried to think, to remember. Aeron was never in any of the memories. I don't and can't trust him."

"So? You already said you don't trust anyone."

"I spoke hastily. Like I said, that stone is not Aeron's."

"I don't know what game you're playing, Amanda; I can't believe you!"

"Please, Emily, I can tell you things, things only you would know."

Emily turned away and started back toward the house, disregarding

Amanda's plea.

"I saw him, Em, the man that attacked you, the one that didn't survive!" Emily turned back with a jerk, a tear clinging on her cheek. "I know you were just defending yourself, and you didn't know how it worked yet, just like Kiami didn't know when she kissed that boy."

Emily ran then, but not back to the house as Amanda had thought she might. Instead, she took off into the woods and away from them both as fast as she could.

"I know you saved your friend that day, Em!" she yelled after her, but her words fell flat.

She stood staring at the ground. There was no room for self-pity. She had brought this on herself. Before she realized what was happening, a flutter above her caused her to gasp as Kiami landed gracefully by her feet.

In her haste to be understood, she had forgotten Kiami was perched above them.

Amanda wiped at a tear that streaked down her cheek. "You aren't going to run away?"

Within seconds, Kiami had changed back into her human form. She shrugged but spoke firmly. "I know that you keep secrets from us. I also know that you believe it's for our own good. I guess I now understand how you had watched me on the beach that day."

Before she could pry, Amanda spoke. "I saw what happened to your gem too, and I think I know where it might be."

# 16

## Kiami - Truth Hurts

Amanda explained, "I didn't know until I saw how your necklace amplified your magic in the way it did."

Right now, Kiami had no desire to be reminded further of that day with the boy on the beach. She knew that Amanda was referring to the fact that the boy had wilted in her arms, and she didn't really want to hear it said out loud.

Even before they had moved to the tree line, she had heard the things Amanda said quite clearly, and none of it had really surprised her.

If she understood what Amanda was saying, someone had gifted them the gems in order to amplify their magic.

She had always thought that Jacqueline had left her the moon stone as a birthday present, but if what Amanda was implying was true, she had been wrong about her guardian all along.

Kiami had believed the necklace fell off during the encounter on the beach, when Jacqueline had seen what happened to the young man she had kissed.

It had all happened so fast.

Kiami's stomach had twisted with the questions that bloomed in her mind. What if Jacqueline had been reacting to the gem and not the fact that she seemed to drain the life from some unsuspecting person? Had she been trying to take the necklace during the scuffle, and if so, had she done it to help her or hurt her?

She pushed the thoughts from her mind, and the twisting in her stomach subsided. There was no way for her to know for sure unless she was reunited with her guardian, so it would do no good to dwell on it.

She shook her head, indicating to Amanda that she didn't need to explain. Then she reached for her hand and walked with her into the woods to look for Emily.

She didn't want to make Amanda feel better about keeping the visions from her. In fact, she wanted to be mad, but she understood what not being trusted felt like: it hurt.

She had experienced it that day Jacqueline had accused her of making her mom sick, and for her, it was a pain that never subsided.

"I know what it's like to need someone to trust you and see in their eyes that they are not willing to."

She knew it had been fear that stopped Amanda from telling them about the visions in the beginning, but what she feared most about them, Kiami wasn't sure.

As they approached, Emily made no move to run. She sat still on the rotten log she had chosen for contemplation. She didn't even make a face in acknowledgment of their arrival. She just continued to draw lines in the dirt with a broken stick she had picked up.

Kiami sat beside her and rested her hand against her back, comforting her. "Em, we have all had to do things we aren't proud of."

Emily looked at her then. "I killed him," she croaked.

"I know, it's okay." Kiami wrapped her arms around. "Emily, you need to listen to Amanda. I don't think she's lying. I'm not proud of some of the things I have done, but I take solace in knowing the torments that we have had to endure have not been for nothing."

"I'm frightened, Kiami. The truth may be scarier than anything we imagined."

Emily looked up and addressed Amanda. "What does he want?"

"I don't know, but we need to find out. Maybe he just wants what Abaddon wanted."

"And what was that?"

"Basically, he wanted me dead. I think to make sure that we couldn't find each other. He said I should save him the trouble by killing myself... And I would have." She looked away, ashamed. "It's why Aden sacrificed himself."

Emily spoke in a soft, tired voice. "What can we do?"

"Jacob. URD. Abaddon. I think they were puppets. We have to find the puppeteer."

"Doesn't that make us puppets too?" Kiami suggested.

Amanda looked back at her with her eyebrows raised. Jacob had once referred to her as a puppet, and she hadn't liked it at all.

"If we were acting like puppets, whoever is controlling this wouldn't be trying so hard to pull us apart."

Emily dropped her stick and raised her voice. "We need to tell Justin."

Amanda shook her head. "If you tell him my theory, he will never believe it."

Emily kicked at the dirt and then looked back and forth between Kiami and Amanda. "You know, I think he latched on to Aeron the way he did because he felt that Aeron could see things more easily from his perspective. Have you noticed how he keeps complaining that we gang up on him?"

Kiami nodded. "Now that you mention it. I have, yes."

"I think have an idea that may help."

Curiosity bloomed within Kiami. If Emily had a plan, now was the time to speak up. "What is it?"

She chewed at her bottom lip for a few seconds, as if she was afraid to say it. "What if we show him by taking him to go check on the townspeople? If you are right, Amanda, and Aeron is an imposter meaning to do harm, then in theory, he won't be able to follow us through the barrier into the town."

Amanda nodded, adding, "Good idea."

Kiami spoke up. "I think it's a great idea, but we can't let Aeron know we suspect anything — and what about the other one, Etzion?"

"I will stay behind with him in case he wakes up. Justin will be more at ease without me there anyway," Amanda offered.

Kiami agreed, but she was still worried about Aeron catching on. The only way she could think to help would be to spy. "I'm going to say that I will stay behind with Amanda. It's just a precaution. I can follow in owl form, and if anything goes sideways, I can help."

# 17

# Emily - Vanishing Act

She had wanted to stay angry with Amanda for leaving her in the horrible situation at home, but she reasoned with herself it had been her own cowardice that had kept her there as long as it had. And when she had stopped being angry, she had seen Amanda's perspective a little more clearly.

It had been Amanda's earlier reluctance to go into town that had given her the idea of doing just that with Aeron. If he slipped through the barrier unaffected, she would know that Amanda's fears had been unfounded, and if he didn't, she hoped Justin would catch on.

Emily saw a small movement toward the wooded area and looked in that direction, noting the light gray and silver wings outstretched as an owl watched from above. She moved along the road that led to town hoping Kiami would not reveal herself, and feeling slightly better that she would, in fact, be rather close by.

It hadn't been all that hard to get Aeron to agree to join her and Justin to check on the jinn village. He had seemed a little surprised by the invitation.

For most of the walk, she had been reeling from the idea that Aeron could be an imposter, but now, as they got closer to the town limits she was a little surprised to feel excitement bubbling up underneath her worry.

The boys had been laughing at something earlier as the girls returned from the woods. Seeing the look on Amanda and Kiami's faces had made her think that the trio, herself included, would have a problem trying to keep their cool.

At first, as they sat around the table, Emily looked numbly past the accused imposter, afraid to speak for fear of letting him know that they had found him out as he and Justin chatted back and forth about random nonsense.

But the longer she attempted to keep her eyes from settling on Aeron, the less she seemed able to stop herself, and Amanda kicked her leg under the table, reminding her not to stare.

After that, she tried resting her chin on her hand to avoid eye contact. But to her dismay, Amanda kicked her again much harder.

She grabbed her leg as she cried out, "Ow."

"Oh, Em. Are you alright?" Amanda muttered sarcastically.

She widened her eyes and turned them on Amanda as she mouthed, "What?"

Amanda shrugged with a lopsided grin. "Didn't you want to go to town?"

Justin shifted his gaze in her direction. "I thought we decided it wasn't necessary."

Emily crinkled her brow as she moved her eyes from Justin to Amanda and back. Realization dawned on her. The staring hadn't been the reason for Amanda's assault on her; she had wanted her to speak up.

She looked down at her hands and fidgeted as she spoke. "I am really worried about Gemma and Cherry."

He tilted his head to the side, a question lingering in his eyes.

"It's just the state of the forest has me wondering how the village made out. You really have to see it to believe it."

Worry clouded his features. "Is it really that bad?"

She nodded.

"Then we should walk. We will get a better idea of the destruction on foot, and if there could be obstacles in the road, we won't have to move them right away."

In truth, even though she had been shocked the night before by Justin saying he wasn't worried about his family, she hadn't been all that nervous about the town's condition, at least not before they started to get close to the barrier. The townspeople were magical creatures, after all.

But as they moved onward, patches of the earth seemed to be missing, ripped clean of plants and dried up.

It reminded her of the day she had crossed the stream and tumbled into town. How strange it had been to witness the shallow bank on the dehydrated side, and on the other bank, mere feet in front of her, a thick blanket of grass had covered the ground, and flowers dotted the landscape.

Only instead of a clear boundary that the water had created, between the desert-like environment and the field that buzzed with life, there were whole areas of barren earth everywhere, some small sections and some larger that intertwined with patches of lush grass and flowers in complete contradiction, as if one landscape was trying to consume the other.

Emily pondered if the storm had done this, or the jinn.

Aeron had been jabbering the whole way, but she had paid little attention to the things he said. For the most part, it sounded like he was reiterating the previous night's events.

Justin hadn't said much since they began their walk, but he smiled on, nodding eagerly at most of the things Aeron spewed from his mouth.

If she had to guess, she would say that Justin already had some idea of what she was trying to prove, but was convinced of his new friend's character.

Emily wandered the area where she knew the entrance to town should be. She moved her foot across, testing it, much as she had with the stream that first day, but with more confidence.

She had never felt so much as a tingle when she crossed the barrier before, and she didn't now, but would Aeron?

She had inadvertently walked a distance ahead of them and would have turned back if not for the lack of noise that seemed to surround her.

No birds chirped, no wind rustled the leaves, and as the pair approached her, she realized even though she could see their mouths moving, she couldn't hear their banter anymore. It was as if she had used her fingers to plug her ears. It made her blood run cold.

Overwhelmed by dread and knowing that she wouldn't truly be leaving Justin alone with Aeron, she took off at a dead run to the diner, hoping that Kiami would stay close to the pair instead of following her.

She was panting and out of breath by the time she reached the doors to One Last Bite.

She pushed them open and stared inside the unlit restaurant for a moment. Then she turned on her heels and raced on, glancing in doors and windows all the way down the street until she reached Gemma's shop. She put her face against the glass and peered into the dark windows.

Were they still hiding out from the storm? By all appearances, it looked like they had abandoned the town.

She jogged across the street and entered the bookshop in such a rush that the opening and closing of the door created a small gust, toppling the pile of magazines that had been stacked closest to it. Frustrated at seeing no one at all, Emily lowered herself to the floor, questioning if they could be hiding.

Jinni had the ability to be unseen, and that she knew of, only Amanda could see past that ruse. But surely, she thought, they wouldn't hide from her.

She ran her hands through her hair and hung her head as her mind shifted through possible explanations. Had they all died and turned to dust, as she had learned jinn did?

A hand grasped her shoulder. *Have you lost your mind?* It was Justin's voice that nudged her back to her feet, his eyebrows lifted as he questioned her, and his mouth set in a worried grin. The voice was coming from within her own head. *Take another gander around,* he offered.

She had no doubt he had seen her terrified expression and noticed something she had not. She walked around the familiar room and stopped at the wall where the door to the underground area had been, running her hand over the now smooth surface.

He reached out and grabbed her hand. He gave it a gentle squeeze before relaxing his grip but didn't let go. *The magic I'm using to communicate with you will only work one way, and I must be touching you for you to hear me. I tried to call to you before you ran off, but it was too late. You were already within the town's shield. The magic that protects this place has different responses for different perceived threats. It will return to normal once the threat leaves.*

Justin pulled her at her arm. *Let's get out of here.*

Now that the initial shock at seeing the empty village had been nullified by the implication that the jinn had somehow sealed themselves below the bookstore, Emily found herself a bit confounded by the idea that Justin had an ability, it seemed, that she hadn't known about.

She pondered her new knowledge as he pulled her along. She supposed he hadn't had a reason to show her this particular talent before. Or, she realized, maybe it was hard for him and he was embarrassed, like the time he had made her look away when he had trouble using his magic to ignite a simple flame.

When they reached the edge of town, Emily released his hand and leaned in, closing the gap between them before speaking in a low tone she hoped only Justin could hear. "You could have warned me."

He raised one eyebrow at her and then bent down in close to her ear. "If you told me what you were trying to accomplish by coming here, I would have."

As he stepped away, Emily threw him an apologetic smile, but he didn't seem to notice.

He had already refocused his attention on Aeron, who was lying still on the cracked pavement.

Justin cleared his throat. "Are you feeling better?"

"No," Aeron responded, throwing his arm across his face in a gesture of agony.

Justin kicked at some rocks as he shuffled toward him, and Emily knew there wouldn't be a need for explanation; his confidence in Aeron had been shaken.

Emily knew he must have stepped over the barrier and turned back at the first signs of discomfort. He may have even offered to stay outside and keep a lookout, but that wouldn't fool Justin.

An owl soared above them, and Emily was relieved that Kiami didn't bother trying to hide anymore.

# 18

# Amanda - Etzion

The others were walking to town, which meant it could be hours before they got back, depending on how long they stayed there.

After they had left, Fizzle abandoned his post outside and followed her up the stairs, almost prancing behind her with excitement.

Time seemed to tick by slowly as Amanda watched over Etzion. He had begun to move around in his sleep, tossing the covers to the floor and turning onto his side.

She took this as a sign that he had been sufficiently healed for him to wake, and she attempted to rouse him by placing a hand on his shoulder and shaking it gently. "Etzion. Get up."

When his eyes remained closed, she added a little more force to her hand and her voice. "Etzion."

Just as she was about to give up, Fizzle jumped onto the bed, growling softly, and with a sudden jerk, the young man jolted up into a sitting position.

His eyes were large, round circles, and his chin quivered.

Amanda stayed still, waiting for him to acknowledge her. She didn't want to startle him further.

Fizzle let out another low *grrrrwwl* and moved in a circle on the bed.

Etzion's shoulders relaxed as he looked at the critter and reached out to pat it. A slow smile crawled up one side of his mouth and then dropped as his eyes latched onto her.

Amanda took a slow step forward. "How are you feeling?"

"I don't... I'm not sure. How did I get here?"

"I was hoping you could tell me that."

He reached up and rubbed at the back of his neck as if it were sore. Fizzle had moved onto his lap and now stared up at him with a small portion of his tongue hanging out.

Etzion raised his hand as if to pet him again but stopped halfway. "It isn't going to bite me, is it?"

"Fizzle?" Amanda shook her head, "I doubt it, try to lick you maybe. Don't let him, though."

He raised an eyebrow at her but patted the creature again.

She moved closer to the bed and offered an explanation. "It seems that his saliva can have some mood-altering effects."

"I see. Not quite the weirdest thing I have heard lately."

"So, you do remember?"

"I..." He dropped his hand to his side and pushed himself up straighter, causing Fizzle to jump off the bed. "I came here to find you."

"Me? But why?" Amanda held up her hand. "Wait. Let's start over. Tell me how you ended up with Aeron."

He shrugged. "Wishful thinking, I guess. I knew there was a reason for my ability, but I never really questioned it. I didn't need to, ya know? It's like I knew eventually I would find out its purpose, and my gift was easy enough to keep a secret. I mean, my mom knew about it."

Amanda offered a slow nod of understanding.

"But then he showed up one day."

"And you just went with him?"

"I assumed he was what I was waiting for." His forehead creased more as he tilted his chin up at her. "If he is the bad guy, then you must be the good guy, right?"

She wished things were as simple as that. "Before I can attempt to answer, I need you to tell me how you ended up almost dead here on our doorstep."

He looked down at the blanket for a moment, as if reading off a list there. "He told me I was only half human, and that's why I have my gift. He said that he needed to find the others like me and that I could help him. He also said your name was Amanda. He described you pretty well, and he told me about the others." He looked up at her expectantly. "Where are they?"

"They are out there on the road with him now, checking the damage of the storm. That's why you need to tell me what you know."

"Just that he got me to go with him."

He lowered his eyes as if shamed or embarrassed. "I questioned little things he said and did, but it was the blue smoke creatures that tipped me off."

"The wisps?" Amanda questioned.

"Is that what you call them?"

She nodded. "That's what we have come to refer to them as."

"Makes sense. They are little wispy balls of smoke. Or at least that's what they appear to be..." He trailed off for a moment, as if a new thought had occurred to him. "Anyway, they swarmed before the storm started."

Amanda lowered herself onto the edge of the bed. "Tell me what happened, exactly."

The lines on his forehead diminished as his expression changed from one of shame and concern to concentration. "I think maybe he chose me because he had been hoping that if he told me about each of you, I could teleport him to you. But it doesn't work like that. I need to have been somewhere, then I can call the image up in my mind and transport back."

Amanda nodded; that was her thinking when she had witnessed him traveling in her visions.

"Even after I explained it, he still insisted that I go with him. Like I told you, I always knew there was a reason for my gift, so I didn't question it." He closed his eyes and leaned his head back. "Until last night, our journey was pretty uneventful. We had only been traveling for a few days." He moved his hand to his chest and winced. A low wheeze escaped his mouth.

"Are you okay? Do you want some water?"

He rocked his head from side to side. "Let me explain first."

He grimaced as he pushed himself back up into a full sitting position. "We were on the road. We couldn't have been too far from here when the old man jumped out of the woods."

"Old man?"

"Yes. He ran at us, hunched over and hobbling as he moved. When he got close to Aeron, I looked into his eyes. They were strange. Gray, vacant. I want to say almost the same color as his hair, but it was matted and dirty, as were his clothes."

Amanda rubbed at her exposed shoulder until she felt the raised bumps of the scars that Jacob had inflicted on her. "Maybe he had been in the woods for a long time," she said.

Etzion shrugged one shoulder. "When he reached us, I could hear him babbling about gardens of children and crying statues. He was ranting like a lunatic, and Aeron started laughing at him... That's when the man leapt forward, shouting as he wrapped his hands around Aeron's neck. He must have been stronger than he looked, because Aeron couldn't seem to free himself. So I yanked at the man, but his grip was firmer than you would think was possible.

"I stumbled backward, bringing him down with me, and as I grabbed my sapphire from my pocket, the man shrieked and backed away. Something had changed in his eyes; they didn't look as empty. Do you know what I mean?"

Amanda nodded as she folded her arms across her stomach. "Did the man or Aeron say a name?"

"No, he just pointed at Aeron and said, 'You tell him I tried. You tell him.' Then he turned and disappeared back into the woods."

*Jacob? No.* She brushed the thought away. It had been years in the human realm since Aden had left him confused and without his powers.

Etzion drew her attention back as he continued. "That wasn't the weirdest part. It was after I turned around to see if Aeron was alright. The blue wisp creatures were swarming around him."

Etzion leaned in closer to her, clutching at his side. "He screamed at them, calling them pests, and I just backed away."

He paused, his eyes searching her face for understanding, and Amanda relaxed her arms, dropping them back to her sides. "That's the most interesting thing that you have told me so far."

He moved his head in agreement and started talking faster. "I knew they were much more. You may not believe this, but they have helped me in the past. So, when he called the wolves and tried to attack them, I tried to defend them..." He hung his head. "Teleportation isn't very much use against creatures like that. Without my sapphire, I can only transport myself, and I must have dropped it. By then the rain was coming down and the wind had started whipping."

"So Aeron attacked you when you tried to stop him from attacking the wisps?"

Etzion nodded.

Amanda stood up and began walking in slow, deliberate steps back and forth across the room. "If he tried to pass the wisps off as enemies and wanted to destroy them, then they must be a threat to him. Do you know what his plan was after he found us?"

Etzion scowled and shook his head. "I would like to go home. Surely the six of you can handle Aeron."

"Six?"

"Yes, Kiami, You, Emily, Justin, the boy that multiplies himself." He wasn't lying; she had seen him in one of her visions, but somehow she had never managed to catch his name. It seemed that Aeron hadn't known it either.

"Who is the sixth?"

"He referred to the last one as Blaine, but even though he knew his name, he didn't seem to know much about him. Which was strange, because he knew so much about you and the others."

Amanda was only half listening now as she tried to recall a dream she once had, although it hadn't been a dream. She remembered something had pulled her to the dream realm before they had encountered URD, even before Aden had been lost. She had thought it was him that had brought her there, but instead of his familiar face, she had seen something else. Six cloudy figures had wandered the field until they had moved into a semicircle around her. Did those out-of-focus characters represent Kiami, Emily, and the others like herself?

Etzion interrupted her silent contemplation. "I think he has my sapphire."

She sat back on the edge of the mattress, the strange memory of the dream realm still lingering in her mind as she spoke. "We will do what we can to retrieve it. Are you planning on teleporting home?" She scratched at her chin. Aeron seemed to know a lot about her, Emily, Kiami, and even Justin. She had to wonder if it was possible that they were drawing attention to themselves because they were all together. "Go. You will be safer there, and you will recover faster."

She got the feeling that he was better off separated from his stone also, for the time being, anyway. She just hoped that whatever they encountered before his return wouldn't require his help.

"Now that I have been here, I can teleport back to this place," he explained, as if she didn't understand.

Amanda looked at him thoughtfully and clicked her tongue.

"Before I go, I have to ask, Amanda, what makes you trust me?"

She had nothing to hide from him, so she spoke openly. "Because I know you. Etzion, I have spent time with you. I have seen your family." She supposed the last part could be seen as a threat, but she didn't much care. He could take it whatever way he wanted to. Maybe he would keep his guard up from now on.

# 19

# Kiami - The Great Pretender

Kiami had been watching from the trees as they approached the town. Although the place seemed intact, she had noted the odd way the foliage and grass now seemed to only speckle the surrounding landscape, but to her, it was the forest that seemed to have taken the brunt of the storm here as well as back at Justin's.

She had been a bit shocked when Emily took off into the town on her own. It hadn't been what they had discussed. Justin and Aeron had sprinted in after her, but it wasn't long before they had both reappeared outside of the village. Aeron seemed to be retching and heaving, and Justin had been helping by propping him up, as if he couldn't walk normally.

His reaction to the town's protective magic had been much more severe than Aden's had been on the day that she witnessed him sneaking about inside. She wondered if it was because despite his initial distrust of the villagers, Aden's visit hadn't really been malicious.

The tight look on Justin's face told her that he hadn't warned him about the town's magical shield. Justin had helped him back and then vanished into the village himself. The entire time he was gone, Aeron lay with his head on a rock, innocently staring up into the sky.

She almost revealed herself to find out what was up with Emily, but as she watched Justin run off, she was glad she hadn't.

Neither of them were aware that she had been following behind, although she had made it a point to let Emily see her in bird form when they first started out. She figured the best thing to do would be to stay put and keep an eye on Aeron until Justin and Emily returned. At least for now, she had the element of surprise on her side.

When they both reappeared, approaching the outskirts, she had been relieved to see that Emily looked mollified. Just before she had taken off, Kiami noticed a look of sheer terror fill her eyes.

When she had seen Justin kick at some rocks, she decided it was time to show herself, but only to reassure him and Emily that she was close. She would remain in bird form just in case she needed a quick way to reach Amanda if anything went wrong. A shard of doubt lingered as to whether or not they could remain discreet and keep calm all the way back to Justin's house.

She noticed that Emily was trying to make small talk with Aeron, which Kiami thought might not be the best thing, because it was drawing attention to the fact that Justin now wasn't. Her appearance had helped put Emily at ease, but it seemed it did little to reassure Justin. She stayed close, wondering if Aeron noticed the way the roles had switched.

They were only about halfway back from her calculations when she heard Justin mumbling under his breath, like he was coming unhinged. He hadn't known Aeron for long, it was true. But he had given him his trust almost from the start, and he was scolding himself for it.

She wondered if there was anything she could do to snap him out of his apparent stupor and bring him back. She studied the backs of Aeron and Emily, listening to him retell his story yet again.

Because of her exceptional hearing, she had been within earshot each time he told it. Even though it was now clear that he was an imposter, it struck her as odd that there were little to no noticeable changes in his monologue with each telling. It was as if he had rehearsed the lines over and over to be delivered in a certain way.

It wasn't much longer before Kiami's fears were realized.

Whether Aeron would have noticed the change in the pair's behavior since the start or not no longer mattered.

Justin had given up on trying to hold in his anger just as the trail through the woods to his home became visible. She had been watching him as he started to clench and unclench his fists in a dramatic fashion. His face had gone from rosy-cheeked to bright red in what seemed to be only seconds.

He had fallen a few steps behind Emily and Aeron, but there wasn't enough time for her to intervene as she watched him plow forward. She sucked in her breath, waiting for him to attack.

She released it, relieved, as she watched him push between the two of them and move past, racing up the trail. Emily and Aeron watched after him for a moment in stunned silence, and Kiami took the chance to change form within the tree line. In the few moments it took her to change form, it dawned on her that he had raced to the house because he thought that Etzion was also an imposter.

Just as the pair started to move forward again, she raced out of the trees, panting in an exaggerated way. "Em, wait up." She looked at Emily and winked before turning to Aeron, shaking her head. "Boys can be so jealous."

The narrow-eyed look he shot back in her direction told her she wasn't fooling him one bit. Regardless of that, she smiled back at him and reached for Emily's hand. "Let's go talk to him, shall we?"

A chill went down her spine as Aeron said, "Yes. Let's."

She squeezed Emily's hand as they walked. She couldn't help but think that if Amanda had not kept her visions a secret, if she had told them sooner, things may have gone more smoothly.

Amanda stepped out from the cover of the garage as they got closer, with an innocent look pasted on her face.

"Where is he?" Aeron growled.

"I think he's upstairs," she responded politely.

Kiami waited to address her until he disappeared into the house. "I think Justin is looking for Etzion. Instead of picking a fight with Aeron, as I thought he might, he ran here. I believe that after he saw Aeron's reaction at the barrier to town, Justin assumed he would also be a threat."

"Etzion is safe," Amanda offered. "I sent him home after he explained what happened."

Angry words echoed back at the girls from inside the house. "What has she done with Etzion?"

"Does it matter?"

"I think we should get up there," Emily said shakily.

"You should know that he brought me here to help kill you," Aeron announced in his gravelly voice, loud enough for them to hear as the trio jolted up the stairs on their way to the room.

When they reached the open guest room door, they found the pair wrestling on the floor. Both of them had faces colored brick-red from anger and determination.

Justin was in a headlock and Aeron sneered back at him. Kiami assessed the room, trying to determine how best to help Justin. They had knocked the box of memorabilia off the dresser, and as Justin squirmed his way out of Aeron's grip, he stepped on the gift, causing him to fumble forward into the side of the wall with a loud thud.

Kiami looked from him to the package, now split open on the side, the edge of a green gemstone bursting through.

Amanda and Emily's stones both seemed to amplify their magic. She hoped that the same would be true for him.

She plunged forward, grabbing for the box just as Justin managed to push himself back to his feet, screaming, "Imposter," as he pounced at Aeron again.

Before he managed to land his own punch, he doubled over in pain. Aeron was fast. Justin was outmatched. She advanced toward the pair, revealing more of the stone as she clenched the box in her fist. By the time she slapped it into Justin's hand and forced his fingers around it, the stone had come free of its packaging.

She knew he wouldn't understand at first, so she held his hand closed for a moment to allow the him time to realize what she had done. When the confusion finally cleared from his eyes, she let him go and backed away to the hall, where Amanda and Emily stood watching.

Aeron lowered his head and ran at Justin, trying to head-butt him, but before he reached his target, Justin ignited from head to toe. Aeron growled when he made impact and pulled away as the smell of singed hair filled the area.

"Nice move," Amanda whispered in her ear. "But don't you think fire inside is a bad idea?"

"I saw the emerald and just reacted." Her eyes widened as she saw the corner of the blanket that had fallen to the floor erupt into flames. She hadn't helped as much as she had hoped. "What do we do?"

Amanda looked from her to Emily. "You two go outside. Now."

Kiami saw a blur of movement, but didn't move in time. She was shoved out of the way as Aeron bolted down the stairs. She hit the floor with a painful thud as Justin bolted past her and down the stairs, chasing after him.

"Go!" Amanda yelled.

"Not without you."

"I will meet you out there. I can put the fire out."

Kiami glanced back into the now smoke-filled room; the fire had spread to the mattress as well.

Emily tugged at her arm, and she reluctantly followed her down the stairs and outside, leaving Amanda to deal with the growing fire.

Aeron and Justin were staring each other down outside. She was glad to see that Justin still clutched the gemstone in one of his hands, but he was using his free hand to make a come-at-me gesture, and Aeron was imitating him as he started circling him.

Aeron must have noticed their arrival because he bellowed, "Three against one. That hardly seems fair. Let's even things up, shall we?"

"You are pretty cocky for someone that's outnumbered," Justin retorted.

A smile spread across Aeron's face, and he stopped circling. "Who's outnumbered?"

The calmness in his voice made Kiami shudder.

Justin straightened and flicked his hair back from his face nonchalantly. "You are."

A creepy laugh erupted from Aeron's throat. "Look again."

Kiami heard Amanda approaching fast and then stop dead as if she was startled, so she searched the area with her eyes. Large gray wolf-like creatures were moving in from the edges of the forest, ready to surround them.

She knew a look of horror was pasted on her face as she watched Amanda walk past one of the wolves, taking slow steps forward.

Aeron must have notice her too, because he bowed in her direction. "Nice of you to join us."

She replied, "You are awful cocky." As she stepped beside Kiami, she whispered, "Let's circle him."

Kiami nodded and stepped over a few feet to equal out the spaces between them. She glanced up at Emily and saw her do the same.

# 20

# Amanda - Fight Song

Grinning like an idiot, Aeron walked around the interior of the circle they had created, looking at each one of them, scrutinizing them.

Amanda wanted to slap the confident look off his pale face.

"What are you going to do?" he asked, conveying to them that he wasn't afraid in the least.

He thought he could take them all out, Amanda realized, wondering why he believed he was so undefeatable. Was he?

"Who sent you to find me?" she asked in a more demanding voice. "Was it Abaddon?"

"Wow, you are pretty self-absorbed if you think we were only sent after you. Or that Abaddon himself wasn't just a peon. Strong, yes, but not in charge. He only thought he was, much like Jacob."

"Then who?" she urged.

"Be thankful you will never have to meet him," Aeron countered. "Dying now will be so much easier on all of you." His grin didn't falter in the slightest as he spoke, clearly believing every word that left his mouth. "Are you ready?" he questioned, winking at Emily. "Which one of you is going to try to take me down? Your fearful leader here?" He motioned toward her cowering form.

"I'm not..." she began mumbling, and Amanda stepped forward in one quick movement, coming just a few inches from his face. "She is a warrior."

Amanda nodded toward her and was pleased to see that she took a step closer to Aeron too. "And we will bring you down together."

Aeron stood still at the center of them, making no move to escape. He only raised his eyebrows. Amanda didn't wonder why. She knew he thought he had an advantage because they were surrounded by his creatures.

But she had noticed something on her slow approach. The wolves looked identical. They all seemed to be missing the same triangle of matted fur from the left ear, and if that wasn't just a strange coincidence, surely the fact that when he had stopped moving, they also stopped in their tracks, meant something. But was a single wolf to blame, or was it something else? She needed more time.

She spun around to face the one closest to her. Blood lust filled its eyes, and when it bared its teeth at her, so did the one that stood beside it. They were like carbon copies of one image. She pointed her staff at it menacingly, and howls erupted around them.

She turned back to the center, facing Aeron. "This is your army?" She grinned and leaned on her staff, provoking him.

He stepped so close to her, she could hear his slow, steady breath escaping. Beyond him, she could see the wolves move in tighter around them. She lifted her free hand and shoved him back. The wolves flinched and then snarled behind her. "That's what I thought."

She heard Kiami gasp as she reached out to grab Aeron, but he moved out of her way and then straight back at her.

She heard the movement of the wolves as they pounced at that same moment she felt Aeron ram into her with all his force, knocking the air from her lungs. She could taste blood in her mouth as she gasped for breath.

His heavy weight lifted off from her, and she fumbled for her staff. Kiami let out an ear-piercing scream from somewhere nearby, but it was hard to assess her whereabouts. She was surrounded by a flutter of movement. Fur and tails blurred in and out of focus all around her, and at the center Justin and Aeron moved at each other like wild animals.

She inhaled deeply; her chest burned. "Don't bother with the wolves," she yelled as loud as she could above the snarls and yips that echoed around her. "Focus on Aeron." She choked out the words.

Amanda didn't hesitate to strike back. She didn't fixate on the ambushing wolves; instead, she went straight for Aeron at the center of the group.

Justin was ablaze once again, trying to punch and kick at Aeron, but he was so fast, only a few managed to find their mark.

The wind howled suddenly as she drew power through her staff, drawing Aeron's attention to her. She saw the group of wolves pounce on Justin, and she realized her mistake. They weren't just copies of one creature; they were flesh and blood. Something conjured up from Aeron's imagination. Kiami and Emily had been keeping the wolves at bay while Justin and Aeron fought.

She saw them run toward the pile of wolves that now hid Justin from view as Aeron aimed his vengeance at her. The ground rumbled beneath her as she let the wave of magic loose from her staff, and it engulfed him as a pulsing wave of pain hit her abdomen.

She dropped her staff as the pain morphed into a burning sensation within her. Aeron moved closer, the magic dissipating around him. He looked down at her and smiled as she lifted her bloodied hand from her stomach, staring at it in shock.

His smile stretched from ear to ear as she felt her legs fold in under her. She summoned up all the energy she could and said, "Sing." The sound was barely above a whisper when it came out, and as she crumpled to the ground, she hoped it had been loud enough to get Kiami's attention.

She could hear faint movement all around her, but the sound was faded. She tried to force her body into a sitting position, but something other than the pain held her back.

A blur of dark-colored hairs swooshed above her. A firm hand covered her own. She tried to acknowledge Emily, but all that came out was a grunt, and then she felt the strange healing energy radiate all around her. Amanda's eyes fluttered and then closed. A static sound filled her ears, and the burning feeling began to grow duller.

As the sensation of the energy evaporated, she opened her eyes again and allowed Emily to pull her forward. She looked past her savior and released a scream of fury. She scrambled for her staff and pushed herself back up off the ground. Her heart pounded in her chest, and she tightened her grip on her staff until her fingers hurt. She was ready to wipe that smirk off his face permanently.

Then Kiami's song invaded her senses, stopping her in her tracks.

It did nothing to quell the anger that wanted to burst out of her. All she could hear was the melody and her own thoughts as the need filled her to move with the music. She didn't bother to try to fight the urge, but she held on to that feeling of anger with everything she had. She reached for her own magic; it bubbled deep within her.

As she moved with the song, she locked eyes on her target. He swayed along with her, confusion in his eyes.

As the song stopped, she pulled at her own magic, throwing it at him in a way she had never done before. Instead of the slow tendrils of shadowy power she had become accustomed to working with, a ball of inky blackness pushed out, sailing at him and knocking him to the ground.

Amanda moved toward him in such a rush that she barely had time to acknowledge the second wave of power as it pushed at the air beside her. *Emily*, she thought as she jerked her head to the side, stepping out of its path just in time.

Aeron howled as the second force hit him. Amanda saw Justin hovering above him, still covered in flames, unsure of how to move next. She turned around; the wolves lay prone like their master.

She looked back down at Aeron and reached for the dark magic inside her again. This time, it moved out from within her as she expected, in long, shadowy tendrils just as they reached Aeron, wrapping around his limbs as a ball of fire shot forward, covering him.

He seemed to glow beneath the energy of the combined magical attacks. His body withered from its weight. A shrill scream escaped him, making her drop her staff as she reached up to cover her ears with her hands.

Droplets hit her from all angles. She lowered her hands and looked up, but it wasn't raining. Confused, she wiped at the red marks that splattered her skin. They smeared across her flesh with the movement. She breathed in deeply.

The air was heavy with the scent of sweat, fire and, iron. At her feet, a few small balls of fur and globs of flesh lay on the beaten-down grass.

The perfect shape of Aeron's body was burned deep into the ground where he had fallen. There was no sign of Etzion's missing gemstone.

She walked around the area where he fallen again before dropping onto her hands and knees to conduct a closer inspection of the area. When she was satisfied that the sapphire was not there, she leaned back into a sitting position on the ground and tapped her fingers against the exposed dirt as she reviewed her memory of the fight.

Perhaps, she thought, he had dropped it while he was still in the house during his scuffle with Justin.

As she sprang to her feet, she caught sight of Emily and Kiami huddled in a puddle of red liquid, covered in a mixture of blood and dirt. From the looks of them, she would guess that the wolves had managed to gather around them just before they exploded.

She didn't bother to waste time looking for Justin before she spun on her heels and bolted back up to the house in search of the missing gem.

As soon as she entered the doorway, smoke began to fill her lungs. Even though the fire had only been in one room, the whole house had been shut up tight from the storm the night before.

She grabbed a towel from the kitchen and placed it over her mouth and nose. She opened every window that she could on the ground floor before making her way up the stairs and into the guest room.

The whole mattress had gone up in flames before she had managed to get the fire out. She assumed whatever it was stuffed with was perfect food for the flames. All that remained of it was a few pieces of blackened cloth in various spots around the otherwise empty metal frame. The headboard was covered in scorch marks, and the blankets were no more than ash upon the floor. She was lucky she had gotten the fire out as fast as she had. Or rather, she thought, Justin was.

She popped the porthole window open and then swept the floor more thoroughly with her eyes. She crouched down low and looked under the dresser. Sure enough, the gem was there. A weight lifted from her at the sight. She wasn't sure if she would get zapped by the sapphire or not, so she decided to play it safe.

After she wrapped it in the towel that she had been using to cover her mouth, she stuffed it into the top drawer of the dresser so that it could be retrieved later when Etzion returned. It was the safest place, she thought. Even covered in the cloth, she could feel power emanating from the stone.

Without the help of the towel, the smoke began to fill her lungs, and she coughed as she set about making sure she hadn't missed any windows.

# 21

# Emily - A Real Hoot

It was disgusting, warm, and sticky, it was seeping into her clothes, and she could feel it on her flesh. Emily wanted to gag. She had never seen so much blood in her life, let alone had it cover her completely. She swallowed down the feeling. She supposed if she had to endure the sheer torture of it, she could as long as it meant that they were truly rid of Aeron and his pets.

The fight had been rather traumatic from the start, then when they focused on Aeron and he went down, the wolves exploded, spraying red gunk into the air that cascaded on top of them like a sudden burst of rain.

She pinched the bridge of her nose; it didn't smell that great either, but compared with some of the things she had subjected herself to on the road, it was tolerable.

She remembered how once after she had run away, she had looked through trash cans and discovered a fresh pile of squirming maggots and shuddered. Still, they hadn't been all over her.

She closed her eyes and sighed. *I have already survived worse*, she thought to herself, *and I turned out okay.*

For an extra boost of reassurance, she whispered so low that she knew the only person who could have picked up the words was Kiami, "I will endure."

When Kiami failed to acknowledge Emily's remark, she almost repeated the phrase but stopped at the sight of her.

It was the blank stare on Kiami's face that pulled her away from her thoughts, filling her with a new set of worries.

She sat up beside Emily, tears streaming down her cheeks. Her hands fidgeted in her lap. She appeared to be in shock, staring straight ahead and off into the void.

Her powers weren't calling to her, probably, she thought, because it wasn't a physical ailment. Still, Emily wanted to snap her out of it if she could.

She tried to make her voice sound soothing, but it came out a little strained. "Hey, Kiami."

When Kiami failed to respond, Emily moved her hand over Kiami's, stopping the frantic movement she was making with them. They felt cold to the touch.

"Knock, knock."

Kiami whispered back, still not looking at Emily. "Who's there?"

Emily forced out a low giggle just before she responded, "Hoo."

"Hoo who?"

"You sound like an owl."

Kiami turned her eyes up to Emily and gave her a half-smile. "Oh, that was really bad."

"Yeah, it was; too bad it didn't make you h-owl with laughter," Emily said, stretching her mouth into a grin.

Kiami moved her hand out of Emily's reach. "Okay, let's get serious." The statement came out flat.

Emily zipped her mouth and locked it with an imaginary key, tossing it aside. It had seemed a good excuse to use the silly joke. At least it had helped her lighten her own mood and feel more comfortable with the situation.

Kiami hopped to her feet. This time she didn't whisper. "I mean, WHOOO do you think you are anyway?"

Emily chuckled as she accepted Kiami's help up.

Just as she made it to her feet, Kiami lost her balance, sliding forward in the muck, colliding with her.

When they both landed back where they had begun with a slimy splat, she heard Kiami erupt into laughter, and she couldn't stop herself from doing the same.

Justin's figure appeared over them. "You think this is funny." He threw his hands up in the air. "This is *not* funny."

She tilted her head to the side and looked up at him, biting at her lip to stop herself from giggling more. "I'm sorry. I was only trying to help."

For a moment, she had almost forgotten she was covered in blood.

Justin offered her and Kiami each an outstretched hand, they exchanged a glance and then accepted, allowing him to pull them back to their feet. Once they were upright, Justin turned his back to them and started moving toward his damaged home.

Emily hurried to catch up with him. "I am sorry about your house. Maybe it's not that bad? It can still be your home."

He didn't respond, just picked up his pace as he plowed on ahead of her.

When they approached the entrance, Amanda stepped out of the shadows. "The fire is out, but we can't stay in there tonight."

Her voice sounded a little strained as she added, "I opened all the windows I could. I even pulled the canvas tarp from the broken one in your bedroom just before I came back out here." She started coughing as she pushed the last of the words out.

Amanda leaned forward and placed her hands on her knees as she sucked in more fresh air.

Even though Emily didn't feel her healing magic pulling at her, she asked, "Are you alright?"

She had just healed Amanda and attacked Aeron in such a short amount of time that she wondered if it was possible she didn't feel that urge because right now she just didn't have any magical energy left to use.

Amanda straightened and nodded. "Just inhaled a little too much smoke, Em."

Emily reached up for Justin's hand, but he shook it loose. She had wanted to verify that the town would have returned to normal before offering it up as an alternative. She had thought that he would appreciate being included in the decision. It was, after all, his aunt's house that she roomed in. Embarrassed by the slight, she turned her attention back to Amanda.

Emily knew that she wouldn't be thrilled with the prospect of staying in the town, so even before she got the words out, she anticipated an argument or at least an offer to take them back to the castle instead.

When she opened her mouth to ask, she noted the faraway look in Amanda's eyes as they met hers. "The town, let's go there. We can get cleaned up at my apartment."

When Amanda only nodded in response, Emily crinkled her brow.

"I mean, my area of the house is really just a large bedroom with an attached bath, if that's okay."

Amanda lifted the corner of her mouth in a half smile. "We should talk about Etzion before we go."

## EMILY - A REAL HOOT

Emily toweled the moisture from her hair. They were all on edge during the trip to town, and she had been the root cause.

She felt a twinge of guilt for the way she had let her imagination run rampant. Of course, she had been covered in the blood and gore of the wolves, and that was sure to make anyone feel a bit uneasy, but there was more to it.

Now that she was within the safety of the town, she realized that the paranoia had started to creep in while Amanda was sharing Etzion's story. Most of the tale had been retold in a bland, unemotional manner.

Their meeting, how they had set out on their journey, even the fight between him and Aeron over the appearance of the wisps had seemed almost tame the way she told it, and Emily had felt nothing.

The only point in the story where Amanda had let any emotion slip through was at the moment she described the strange man who had approached them from the woods. She even went out of her way to mention that when she had first heard the tale from Etzion, the man's features had made her think of the sorcerer, Jacob.

She was sure that she had heard a quiver in Amanda's voice. To Emily, she had sounded afraid, and that fear had transferred to her, settling under her skin.

She hadn't realized it was there until Amanda finished the story and Justin insisted that they go to town without the aid of his car.

The others were quick to agree. They could return for his car any time, after all, and it would be easier than cleaning the mess they would make in the vehicle.

Justin had noticed her reluctance right away and gave up his snubbing act to be her hero, insisting he could take on whatever popped out to trouble her.

Although she appreciated the gesture, she found it did little to placate her fears once they were on the open road.

At one point, she even insisted to the others that she had seen silvery, frantic eyes watching from the tree line, but a closer search from Justin hadn't revealed a single sign that anyone or anything was following them.

After his investigation, she noticed that she was no longer the only one who jumped as the fallen leaves crackled and crunched beneath her feet.

Justin stuck close by her side the rest of the way, and although Amanda had moved ahead of them on the road, she glanced back at the pair every few minutes.

She had managed to make them all discontented with her wild ideas.

*Can't change that now*, Emily thought as she threw the clothing she had been wearing during the battle with Aeron into the trash.

She envied the fact that Kiami hadn't had to traipse down the road covered in the remains of the wolves. She had transformed into an owl for the journey to town, and when she had changed back, she looked refreshed. Clean. By the time they started the trip, the gore had dried to Emily's skin, making it feel itchy and uncomfortable.

Now, she studied her face in the mirror, smiling, happy to be free of the filth.

Once they arrived, Justin had insisted Nina wouldn't mind if they used the other rooms in the house, but Kiami and Amanda both decided to stay in Emily's room, not caring if they had to sleep on the floor. Even though she knew deep down that Amanda hadn't wanted to come here, she was relieved that they were all together.

When she made her way out of the bathroom, she wasn't surprised to see that the three of them were waiting for her, eager to discuss the next course of action.

Amanda was convinced there was truth in some of the things that Aeron had said, and she wanted to prove it to them. She had explained her gem theory to the others, and when asked, Emily couldn't deny that she had seen a sapphire like Etzion's or an emerald like Justin's in the painting.

She figured the best way to weed out the lies and seek further proof was to obtain Kiami's missing stone. Then none of them, she had reasoned, could brush it off as coincidence. Since Justin's unopened gift had proved to be what she had feared, Emily couldn't disagree with her thinking any longer.

There was no denying that the emerald wrapped in the package had boosted his abilities during the fight with Aeron.

Amanda knew of a tomb of lost things; in fact, she claimed to have found her own missing gem there at one point. Emily felt fine about that. It seemed just as plausible as the other things she had learned since discovering the jinn village.

It was the step after that destination Amanda proposed that made her apprehensive.

The first time she had traveled from the human realm into the Arcane realm had been sort of fun, as new experiences sometimes are, but since they had returned, she felt reluctant to go on a journey of that nature again. In fact, she didn't think any of them should go.

It was something she felt inside of her, akin to when she had known that Kiami was in danger when she was dragged back to the Arcane realm by Amanda. She wasn't sure if it was something deeper, just fear, or if she just didn't like traveling through the veil that separated them.

She simply knew she didn't want them to find Bloise. She even offered to stay behind, in the hopes that it would dissuade them.

Her offer had thrown the others for a loop. She was the one, after all, that had kept insisting they remain together earlier on.

Amanda shook her head and rolled her eyes at the suggestion. "No, the four of us go. Kiami needs to come with me to the tomb. For one, I can't retrieve her missing item without her. Or at least, it is my belief that only she can find it because it belongs to her. Besides that," Amanda added, "we may also need to make a bargain with Bloise and already have the attention of whatever is causing this."

Emily countered, "What about Etzion?"

"I already explained that. His gem is at Justin's, and I think he is safer without it until he is fully himself again. Let's keep him out of the spotlight as long as we can."

"Aeron found him."

"Yes, but Etzion won't be so quick to go with anyone else, and if someone does come looking, he will just teleport back to Justin's."

"Then someone could stay to wait for him."

Amanda shook her head again. "No. Where is this coming from, Em?"

"I don't think we should go see Bloise. It's a feeling I have."

"He might have my mom's journal, Em. Listen, we are all afraid of something, no?" Kiami offered a half smile but dropped it when Justin turned to look at her, glaring as she added, "Justin's not fond of spiders."

Emily looked away but nodded, wondering why she hadn't known that Justin had arachnophobia. "We are stronger together. I get it." She swallowed hard. Maybe, she thought, deep down she was worried that all of Amanda's theories were correct, even the one about the barriers weakening with each use of the stones. If it was the truth, it would help to explain why the jinn had continued to hide.

Amanda placed a hand on her shoulder, causing her to look back up as she addressed them all. "So we agree? We go to the tomb and then continue on to see Bloise?"

As Kiami and Justin walked out of Emily's small home to prepare, she looked up at Amanda. She could see excitement dancing in her eyes.

What Amanda had said to Aeron before the fight had been weighing on her; she certainly didn't feel a speck of bravery right now, and she wanted to ask her about it while they were alone.

"Amanda?"

"Yes."

She folded her arms over her chest but spoke barely above a whisper. "Why did you say that to Aeron, the thing about me being a warrior?"

Amanda grinned back at her. "Because you are. Beneath that exterior, it's there."

Emily bowed her head. "You are wrong, Amanda. I am not a warrior."

"Because you are scared?"

She nodded.

"Remember what Gemma said to me about being lost before we went down below the bookstore?"

Emily nodded again.

"Since then, I have tried to remind myself of the words she used over and over. And I want you to do the same with what I say now."

"Okay."

"Were you scared when your friend jumped off that diving board and hit her head?"

She mulled it over for a moment. "I don't remember. I just reacted."

"I will bet my life that you were. You were scared that she would die. It's how you react to that fear that proves you are a warrior." She reached her arm around Emily's shoulders. The excitement had drained from her voice as she pushed her point. "Emily, even if you couldn't have saved her, it wouldn't have made your actions any less heroic."

She knew it was hard for Amanda to get so personal; it didn't come as easily for her as it did Kiami. That's why her words meant a lot to Emily, even though she knew Amanda was still tormented by the loss of her own friends, the ones she hadn't been able to save. She was still very convincing.

Amanda lifted her arm from Emily's shoulders. "You will see."

## 22

## Amanda - Wrong Turn

A loud whirring hummed in Amanda's right ear, and she swatted in its direction in annoyance. The air smelled stale, like they were in a poorly ventilated enclosure, yet they were out in the open. This was all wrong.

She turned in a circle, trying to get a better look at the strange place they had ended up appearing. Rocks jutted up out of the ground at odd angles, a bark-less tree loomed eerily above her, and small clouds of black flying insects lingered, hovering and emitting an annoying buzz every few feet in all directions.

Amanda had to wonder if they were the biting kind as she counted to make sure that all four of them were in fact present.

The trio looked back at her, and she knew they were expecting her to say something. She moved to step closer to them, and as she placed her foot down, she heard a strangled gasp and a soft crunch.

She lifted her foot and looked down at the broken flower she had trampled. A musky scent rose up into her nostrils. She squatted to scrutinize the purple and red remains at her feet, but the plant life was too mangled to properly investigate. She saw another a few steps ahead and made her way toward it. Heart-shaped black petals ringed the grayish mound, and at its center was a solid black dot that looked like the center of an eyeball.

Curious, she brought her finger as close to the center part as possible, meaning to poke it. The petals suddenly folded in around the eye, blocking her intrusive prodding.

She poked at the petals instead. They didn't feel thin and soft, but rather thicker and waxy like a leaf. She ran her finger gently over the shiny petal, and sure enough, vein-like lines could be felt beneath her fingertips.

Before she knew what her hands were doing, she probed the leaves lower down on the stem. They didn't feel soft and delicate either, but rough, with tiny bristles along their edges. The leaves were almost triangular, broad at the base, with the tip tapering to a rounded point.

Justin scolded her. "Those flowers could be poisonous; we don't know."

She nodded as she stood but kept her eyes trained on the specimen. "I suppose they could be."

The petals unfolded, and Amanda took a step back, sure that the plant creature's eyeball was set on her. She took another step away while watching, and sure enough, the center seemed to twitch and move.

"Do you guys see this?"

"Bizarre is what they are," Emily said. "They can't really be plants, can they?"

It was an interesting question, although one she didn't think she could answer.

While they were hiking or exploring, Amanda and her father had often taken time to learn about the plants they had stumbled across, but she was no expert botanist.

"They look like flowers to me." She shrugged and moved closer to a patch of them. As she approached, she saw movement at the centers of those flowers too.

She stared down at them, unnerved that they didn't seem to blink. She waved a hand over them, and just as she was expecting, they all closed up tightly. *Maybe that is the way they blink,* she wondered. Would it bleed if she picked one? The thought of plucking one to find out seemed wicked. If it bled as an animal did, that would be cruel. She wouldn't take the chance of leaving it with blood oozing from its stem.

She could describe the scene laid out in front of them in one word: wrong. This place was chaotic to her. Somehow, they had gone astray. Instead of merely traveling to the tomb as she had planned, it appeared that they had passed into another realm.

"So, where's the tomb?"

Amanda looked up at Justin. "Not here."

"What do you mean not here?" he countered.

Amanda tried to keep the annoyance she felt toward his questions from creeping into her voice and failed. "I thought it was pretty obvious that we are no longer in the human realm."

"Well then, what are we doing? We should go back."

"Don't you want to know where we are?"

She ignored him, consumed with curiosity she trotted ahead, not heeding cautions as she had been warned to do. It was another much louder crunch beneath her feet that put her back on alert. This time she had trampled over a pile of sun-bleached bones.

Upon further inspection around her, she saw what appeared to be small piles of animal bones of various shapes and sizes hidden amongst the colorful vegetation. The ones she had stepped on were much larger than the others. They looked human-like.

As the others moved toward her pointing, she gawked at the frail white bones that were stripped of flesh, muscle, fat, blood, and tendons. The hair on the back of her neck prickled.

Some old ragged clothing pieces could be seen beneath the incomplete skeleton. She heard Emily breathe in sharply. The scene painted a grim picture. Amanda moved away, swearing she was going to pay closer attention to where she walked from now on.

"What do you think did this?" Kiami asked, folding her arms over her chest as if she was trying to stop a chill.

A short distance to the right, next to a ridged and fragmented vertebra, was a pair of large leather boots that seemed barely worn. A thick brown barkless tree vine or thin tree root ran along the top of the ground beside the remains, and Amanda followed it to its source. A large mound that looked like the buried cap of a mushroom protruded up from the soil, bright red plate-size circles dotting the otherwise crème-colored plant. Here she could see that several of the long vines snaked out around it, spreading in various directions.

Emily asked, "How long do you think those bones have been there?"

The worry was evident in Justin's voice as he responded. "They could have been there for days, weeks, months, years, or maybe only hours. We can't stay here."

Amanda added, "It would be hard to say how long they have been here, Em. At least without an intimate knowledge of what had happened to them and how the environment would have affected them." It was something she had heard her father say about biological items they had stumbled on when they were hiking.

Justin spoke again. "That's what I'm getting at. For all we know, the early morning mist is acid that erodes away everything it touches. I'm not saying it is, just that we can't say that it isn't. We don't know anything about this place."

Amanda agreed somewhat. If she was right, and this was the Chaos realm, they were certainly putting themselves in danger by being here. Hadn't URD said that her master and herself had originated from this odd place of existence, after all?

They could just leave, run back to the human realm, and go get Kiami's stone as they had planned. She could use her staff to make another attempt at the trip, but using her stone really did seem to be making things worse, and maybe there was something important here to find, she thought. On the other hand, there could be nothing at all.

Justin made a squeak as one of the thick vines rose in front of her, blocking her view of him. She could see suction cups running along the underside of the thick vine as it hovered over her.

"It's a tentacle," she whispered just as the mushroom like cap began to lift up from the earth, shaking the soil from its top. Another tentacle rose up beside her, and she held her breath as she assessed the plant creature. It appeared as if the vibrations of their footsteps had caused it to begin to ease its way up from the ground.

With the spotted top no longer resting in the dirt, she could see sharp, pointed spikes stuck out from the gilled underside of the cap that hadn't shown until it lifted up out of the soil, and now she could see that the appendages that had been masked as roots were connected to its wide, solid stalk.

Kiami whispered, "What do we do?"

Two more long tentacles lifted, wavering and twisting, toward them.

Amanda glanced around, not sure how to answer; it seemed like a job more suited for a sword than for magic. A low growl was emitted from somewhere nearby.

"Fizzle?" Kiami cried.

Amanda wondered how he had followed them there. She hadn't seen him since Etzion had returned home. No one had asked since, so she hadn't even spared a thought about the critter.

He moved in blurred circles around the stalk, and after a moment, the tentacles moved in his direction. As fast and sure-footed as he was, Amanda was shocked that he managed to avoid the stalking tentacles' grasp by dodging and weaving this way and that.

"Run," she yelled as she ducked low to avoid an imminent collision with one of the swinging limbs.

They ran forward until the trees of the wooded area vanished from their sight and kept going out into a large open field. She didn't slow down until her heart banged against her chest from the exertion. When they had rushed out into the field, her eyes had locked on to a bridge in the distance, and she had kept going until her shoes had hit the bend of the small lake it stretched across.

As she sucked in her breath, she eyed her surroundings. Here, thin orange and red blades of grass protruded in patches on the ground at the water's edge and reflected back on the surface of the shoreline. As the water rippled out, it looked almost like a spectral fire burned beneath the top layer of liquid.

In front of them, the bridge bent in a perfect half circle above what appeared to be the centermost point of the lakelet. It was also reflected back at her, making it appear as a perfect circle to the eye at first glance. Like the black tower she had encountered in the jinn realm, it was an architectural marvel.

The steep arch of the stone construct was covered in tiny flowers and slender purple vines that hung down, almost touching the water. The construction of such a bridge had to have been a feat of some ingenuity or magic.

Either way, it seemed like it was no longer in use by humans or magical beings. Moss and bugs crawled freely around the gentle curve. The creatures looked like your average cockroaches and beetles, but she knew better than to make assumptions. She scolded herself for the attack. She should have known better than to presume she didn't need to be on guard at all times.

She couldn't help but speculate about the bridge. She was curious to know if it could hold her weight or if the stones would crumble the moment she placed herself upon it. Was it worth the risk to climb those steps and move across, only to have the beautiful creation destroyed under them and to crash land in the water anyway? Who knew what things lurked just beneath the surface?

They had already encountered enough odd things here... and they had been lucky in their ability to remain unscathed. But luck could only bring them so far. She just couldn't help it. It was still in her nature to be inquisitive, even after all she had learned.

Emily plopped down on the ground and patted it with her hand. "Maybe we should sit here a moment."

Amanda turned in a circle, scanning the field. They hadn't caught a glimpse of a single little four-legged critter scurrying along their path as they ran, or even birds in the sky for that matter.

She didn't see any of the peculiar watching flowers here, but off in the distance on either side of the lakelet, she could make out more of the spotted mushroom caps. She hoped that they were far enough away not to disturb them.

"Should I make a fire?" Justin asked.

Amanda shrugged. They knew nothing of this ecosystem, and everything they had encountered had a very deceptive appearance. "I think we should stay for a while. But I don't think that we should chance eating anything that grows here. To be honest, I am a bit leery of making a fire. We don't want to piss these creatures off, do we?"

Justin dropped his shoulders. "Why wait here at all then? Let's get to the tomb and get it over with."

Amanda wrung her hands. "I think we are weakening the veil with each use of our gems. I believe it's why our trip didn't work right. Three of us had our stones help in the fight against Aeron, and look where we ended up the first time. I tried to use mine to aid in our travel." Justin gawked at her in disbelief, so she added, "At the very least it proves that our stones affect the barrier one way or another. You can't deny it. So we wait for a bit, unless you can now manage travel through the realms that is." Justin turned away from her and stared out into the water.

"Did you at least determine where we ended up?" Emily asked.

"Best guess? The Chaos realm."

Justin turned back in their direction with a jerk. "That's crazy."

Amanda pushed herself to her feet. "You know what, I am sick of hearing that. Where else could such things live? Remember the story, how everything left over was thrown in—"

Emily interrupted. "We do know that there is a functioning society somewhere in the Chaos realm."

"Yeah, a dangerous one, apparently," Justin quipped.

Emily raised her voice a notch as she responded, "We can't assume that everyone in the Chaos realm is like URD and Abaddon."

Kiami glanced over her shoulder at them. "Aren't we going to give Fizzle a chance to find us again?"

"Am I the only one that wants to leave?"

Amanda thought that Justin sounded annoyed and hurt as he spoke. His tone didn't improve when he addressed Kiami. "I thought you were used to the way that teleporting, realm-hopping, fuzzball jumped in and out of our lives."

"Fine." She stepped closer to him but stared up at the stone structure. "I want to see what's on the other side of that bridge." Her voice sounded whiny as she protested.

Amanda looked doubtfully up at the bridge. "Surely, there is a safer way around. I don't think the potential consequences of walking over it would be worth the risk."

Emily offered, "Maybe a short swim to the other side. Wet clothes might be bothersome, though."

Kiami shook her head. "No, thanks."

To Amanda's surprise, Emily offered another solution. "If you are so set on it, why not fly over to the other side, and we will wait here?" Unlike Justin, she thought it was a good idea. She hoped that whatever Kiami found on the other side would help to quell her own curiosities. As a group, they weren't well prepared to go exploring.

Amanda started picking at the red and orange blades of grass. She should have thought through the trip better. She should have planned for wrong turns. Her father would have been disappointed in her. *Be ready for anything*, he used to say. All she had grabbed was her staff and a satchel that held robes for their trip to find Bloise.

# 23

# Emily - Cry Wolf

Emily needed a breather. She leaned back on the palms of her hands and looked into the field as Kiami and Justin's chatter continued behind her at the water's edge.

She hoped Kiami would take her idea of flying over the bridge into consideration. She didn't know why Justin was so dead set against her doing a little exploring. She was certain that Kiami was capable of taking care of herself. It wasn't like she would be that far away.

The flash of something bounding around the field caught her eye, and as it moved forward and then back, a smile sprouted on her face.

Although it was still too far away to make out its features, she could see the outline of its shape as it moved. It appeared to be a canine of some sort. It looked like the animal was playing as it zipped around, chasing something small, like a butterfly or a bug of some sort.

The animal stopped and bent the front of its body down. A long tail rose up and began to fan back and forth. It stayed in that position for several seconds before it pounced forward.

It must have missed whatever tiny thing it was hunting, because it jumped back up and ran in a circle, continuing the pursuit.

This was the first freewheeling creature she had seen since they had arrived, and she looked on in wonder at how the animal could romp so freely in a place that seemed to hold so many hidden threats. She tilted her head to the side. She supposed if you were accustomed to the things that lived here and dealt with them every day, the dangers wouldn't seem so severe. She thought of the mushroom plant they had encountered, with its long, flailing tentacles. Maybe the wolf knew ways to bypass the creatures without disrupting them.

She sat forward, aware that the animal was getting closer. It bore similarities to Aeron's pets, but she didn't feel frightened, just curious as the realization sank in.

After all, this animal hadn't followed them from the woods, and before the wolfish army had attacked, she had never had a bad experience with a canine animal before. In fact, this one was so busy frolicking, she didn't even think it had noticed them yet.

She watched the canine creature as it moved in the distance, running closer then stopping, standing stark still, then bounding off in another direction.

"Amanda," she said, keeping her voice low as she turned her head to meet her gaze, "why did you tell us to focus on Aeron and not attack the wolves?"

Amanda tilted her head and released a blade of grass that she had plucked out of the ground from her fingers. "Because they weren't real. From the way they were acting, I deduced that the wolves were something he created from his imagination."

"But what tipped you off?"

She shrugged at Emily. "Well for one thing, the wolves looked identical from ear to tail. At first, I thought that he had a wolf and used magic to multiply it. I have seen something like that before. But then I realized they only moved when he moved or spoke... They were like copies of an image, and they reacted like a single unit attached to Aeron."

She raised her arm and clenched her fingers into a fist, as if reenacting a thought. "If I lifted a hand to Aeron, the wolves flinched and snarled, no matter what direction they were facing."

"But the blood." Goosebumps formed on Emily's arms at the memory, and she crossed them over her chest.

Amanda scrunched up her brow as her face tightened. "It was just the magic he used. Some spells can seem very realistic. Aeron's wolves were made of flesh and blood because they were part of him."

She looked down for a moment and then back up. "They weren't just conjured up either. It was like they were a literal extension of him. I assure you; they weren't really animals at all. They didn't have their own thoughts; they couldn't feel anything on their own. They only felt what he felt and knew what he knew. They were probably modeled after a creature he had seen in passing, maybe something common from where he lived. Maybe he had a bad experience and encounter with a similar animal once and decided it would be a good weapon."

"So you wouldn't say be worried if you saw one around here?"

Amanda smirked at her. "Well, I wouldn't assume it was a bad creature."

Emily shifted her gaze back to the field. The animal had moved closer again on its quest and as if on cue caught her in its stare.

She could see now that the wolf's fur wasn't matted and grungy, like the canines in Aeron's army. Its bright eyes were round and soft. Its demeanor didn't seem threatening at all, but rather very relaxed as it stared straight at her.

It began to juke around, its tail flopping back and forth in an excited motion, as if the animal was asking her to join it on its merry hunt.

Emily glanced back at Amanda. "I am glad to hear that, because there is one watching us now."

Amanda raised an eyebrow at her, and Emily lifted a finger to point toward the wolf in the distance.

Amanda's expression lightened as she looked in the direction of the canine, and Emily was happy to see her lips curve into a smile at the sight. Whatever had been weighing on her mind before Emily interrupted had been temporarily lifted and forgotten as she watched the wolf's wiggling, happy body.

Emily glanced behind her, wondering if Kiami had been listening to their conversation. As menacing as they were, she knew that Kiami had been upset that the poor creatures in Aeron's army had met such a terrible fate. She would have been relieved to know that they were simple manifestations, modeled after something within his mind.

Kiami didn't appear to have heard them; her mind seemed elsewhere. She stood a fair distance from Justin, as if she had wandered away in deep contemplation. Now she was moving back toward him with a new look of determination carved onto her face.

Emily got the impression that the conversation about her going off on her own was about to start anew.

As Justin saw Kiami approaching, he reached down and picked up a small rock before turning away from her.

Emily heard the soft plinks of a stone skipping several times across the water and the light splash it made as it hit the last time before sinking below the surface.

She rolled her eyes and looked back at the wolf, but his ears were now bent down against its head, and his tail was tucked between his legs. His eyes no longer held a playful gleam. He was staring hard, focusing on something behind her in the direction where Justin stood by the water's edge.

The wolf's body had tensed up. Several tufts of fur raised on its hind quarters as it stood there stiff and rigid. Something had scared the canine.

The wolf's eyes stayed glued there as it backed up a couple of feet before it tore them away. It whirled in the opposite direction from them and catapulted forward into the field and out of sight.

Emily furrowed her brow as she looked over at Amanda. "I wonder what spooked it."

Amanda shot her an apologetic look, shrugged, and went back to picking at the grass.

## 24

## Kiami - Right Track

Kiami understood where Amanda was coming from, and she wanted to help. She wondered what the barrier problems could mean for the human realm if they kept using the gems. She supposed if they continued to weaken, unsuspecting humans could walk into another realm, or worse, beings like URD would wander into human cities and wreak havoc.

She sighed and straightened up. Whatever was going to happen to the human realm while they were away was going to happen. The only way that she could see to minimize the impact was to refrain from using the gems, just as Amanda suggested.

She was also hoping that Fizzle would reappear before they left for the tomb, but she knew that even if he did not, there was a good chance he had simply teleported after creating the distraction. It wouldn't be the first instance where he had shown up at the right time and then just disappeared.

She turned on her heels to make her way to the bridge, and Justin reached out to clutch at her wrist. "Don't do it."

Kiami shook his hand off. Even though she was offended and annoyed, she smiled back at him. "Don't you worry about me. I will just fly over and come right back. Maybe I will notice something that will help us to verify where we are."

"It's too dangerous."

Kiami shook her head at him. Helping Amanda stall their departure was only part of her reasoning. She really wanted to see more of this realm. She thought that this was one of the most beautiful places she had ever been. "The forms of life here that we have seen may appear odd or mismatched to us, but it seems to me that they evolved accordingly. They lived and they grew, and they flourished. The seemingly flawed designs work."

He tried to grab for her again, but she backed away before he could reach her.

"Enough of that." Kiami didn't let him get another word in as she transformed and prepared for flight.

After takeoff, she looked down at him. He had his hands on his hips, but he hadn't moved from the spot by the water's edge. She watched for a moment as he bent down and picked something up before throwing it angrily into the water. A rock, she assumed.

She glided forward, watching the water ripple below her as she flapped her wings and flew higher above the arch and across the lakelet to reach the far side.

There was a clear dirt path on this side of the bridge that had green and yellow shrubs running along each side.

Kiami glanced behind her. She knew she should head right back, but instead she stepped forward onto the path and changed back into her human form.

She treaded quietly, listening for the sound of voices. But everything seemed still as she wandered, marveling at the interesting plants.

The straight path led her into an open space that looked like it had purposefully been pruned and maintained in the shape of a circle. Several large piles of leaves and twigs were dumped near the edges, as if someone was in the middle of raking.

She looked around furtively but saw no one. There were seven large bushes that had been pruned and shaped into human-like forms. They took on various poses and seemed to be placed randomly around the interior grounds.

Up ahead across the circular field, she could see what appeared to be the opening of another path. She started to walk toward it, her curiosity pulling at her, when she heard a familiar growl from one of the leaf piles beside her. She stared down at the mound, waiting for whatever was inside to show itself. Sure enough, the debris started moving as a creature crawled out, leaves and twigs clinging to its brown fur. She couldn't stop the smile from stretching across her face.

"Fizzle," she said as she leaned down to pet the critter. "You have to stop doing that. You are going to get hurt."

She wiped the smile off her face and tried to look stern.

Fizzle only danced around at her feet in response. She rolled her eyes and let out a giggle as she patted him again. "Do you want to see what's over there?" She was relieved to see him unharmed.

Just as she was about to walk toward the unexplored trail, a sharp scream echoed across the lakelet, causing her to stop midstride and whip back around in the direction she had come from. She threw an apologetic look in Fizzle's direction and then ran back to the bridge.

If it hadn't been for her exceptional hearing, the noise wouldn't have affected her so. The creature had followed close behind her as she moved. As she stopped at the bridge's edge to change form, she wondered if Fizzle would follow her to the other side in her owl shape.

Another scream rose from the far shore, and Kiami knew that she couldn't take the time to find out. She spread her wings and raced, flying across the lakelet.

Waves of water rushed toward the shore as the giant rock creature walked out from the depths. The lakelet had to be much deeper than it appeared. Kiami could hear stone grinding against stone with each of its heavy steps. The ground rippled with its movements, vibrating with its weight as it hefted itself onto the shore. The thing had to be almost as big as URD had been when it had attacked!

There was no hair or fur, just gray and brown stone. Its coloring resembled that of the bridge, and the monster had moss-covered patches on its body, but they were a darker-colored plant.

She heard Amanda yell, "Stand your ground. Until Kiami gets here."

Emily hollered back at her, "It's just defending itself. For all we know, those little rocks and it are part of the same species."

Kiami could hear a tremble in her voice as Amanda talked through clenched teeth. "I know. Just get closer!"

"Fire isn't going to help!" Emily shrieked.

"Well, what then?" Justin bellowed.

Just as Kiami landed beside them, without a word, Amanda lifted her staff and shadows swirled from the gem, inching their way out in long tendrils. Kiami tried to stay still as they made their way around her body until she was engulfed by them. She turned her head toward Amanda in time to see that they were all embraced by the magic in such a way. She redirected her eyes back to the rock monster; it was almost on them.

The ground shook as it stepped closer, and Kiami had to fight the urge to move out of the thing's path. Its form hovered over them, blocking most of the light from the sky. Kiami's hands trembled as the thing reached down toward them just as they were wrenched up by Amanda's shadow magic and everything turned dark.

Kiami pushed herself up from the ground and dusted herself off. "What the heck happened?"

Amanda looked irritated. Her face was crimson, and she kept one hand balled into a fist at her side. "I got us out of there."

"I know that, but why was that thing attacking?"

"Like it needed a reason," Justin complained.

Amanda turned to look at her and pointed at Justin. "That fool started throwing rocks into the water and wouldn't stop, even after one bit him."

He turned to Emily, as if asking for help, but she only shook her head, refusing to look him in the eye.

Justin made no comment against the accusation, and she was glad. Those two were very good at pushing each other's buttons.

She was disappointed that they had to leave the Chaos realm, but what happened couldn't be undone. "Now what?" she asked.

Amanda kept her voice low. Kiami could practically hear her teeth grinding together as she answered, "Well, the good news is that we are where we need to be this time. The bad news is that I am not sure if we can travel to Bloise's safely afterward."

Kiami shrugged. "We will take it one thing at a time; what else can we do?"

Amanda lifted her cheek in a half smile and unclenched her fist.

That brought a grin back to Kiami's face. Her response seemed to help lighten Amanda's mood, at least.

She took in the barren landscape that surrounded her. It wasn't at all as interesting to her as the Chaos realm had been. *At least the sky is pretty*, she thought. The few wispy clouds that hung against the bright blue back drop of the sky looked like they had been painted on by the most delicate bristles.

Emily looked a little worse for wear, and Kiami wondered if she wouldn't benefit from a few more moments of reprieve before they pushed forward.

"I saw Fizzle on the other side of the bridge. He was in a pile of lawn waste, goofing off as if he didn't have a care in the world."

Emily cast a smile in her direction. "At least we know he got away from the mushroom of doom then."

Kiami nodded. "There were paths on the other side, lined with vibrant shrubbery. I know I was supposed to come right back, but my curiosity got the better of me. I followed one into a clearing that had topiary."

"Topiary?" Amanda asked.

"The designs were all of human forms. I was about to move down the next path when I heard the commotion."

"Sounds like you were putting yourself in danger just being there," Justin blurted. "You don't know what the beings there would do if they found you."

Kiami glared at him. "Neither do you. Stop making assumptions. I'm not the one that got myself attacked."

Justin looked down at the ground and kicked at the dirt.

Amanda glanced in his direction. "It sounds to me like she found another clue that suggests we really were in the Chaos realm."

She turned her attention to Emily. "Remember the picture from under the bookstore? The one you said that you didn't remember seeing before?"

Emily nodded and Amanda continued. "The image of the Chaos realm showed two connecting gardens with a footpath in between: one with the bushes cut into the shapes of people and the other," she paused for a moment as if it eluded her, "had some kind of square carvings. I think they had faces... Did you notice anything else, Kiami?"

She shook her head. "No, sorry." As happy as she was to see Fizzle safe and sound, she almost wished he hadn't interrupted her exploration.

"I didn't see anything like that when I went down there with her."

Amanda turned to Emily. "See, you were right, Em. It was added after you were there with Justin."

The comment caused the corners of Kiami's mouth to lift into a smile. For a moment, she was elated that her journey had not been a waste after all.

Her smile faltered when she heard Justin grumble under his breath, "Can we just get on with this?"

When Amanda spun on her heel to face him, Kiami knew she hadn't been the only one that heard his remark.

She was a bit surprised when Amanda only smirked at him. "Yes, let's."

It hadn't been the reaction to his attitude that Kiami had expected. Maybe, she thought, Amanda was so excited to move forward that she couldn't be mad at Justin.

She watched as Amanda took a few steps forward and motioned for them to follow. "The tomb is in this direction."

Kiami waited to move until they each walked past her. In the distance where Amanda was heading, she could see brown and gray stone walls that protruded up out of the dark-colored dirt.

The entrance had no ceiling, and they could still see up into the sky. On either wall beside her were unlit torches.

Justin and Amanda each grabbed one and lit it using their magical talents.

"You may want to be on the look out for spiders," Amanda said. Her voice sounded playful to Kiami's ears, but the expression on her face seemed to say something else entirely.

She shot a questioning look at Emily, but she only shook her head and mouthed, *I don't know.*

She wondered if Amanda was just trying to get under Justin's skin. She looked around nervously. She wished she hadn't let the thing about the spider at her house slip out.

"You see," Amanda added, "a rather large arachnid landed on me the first time I came here."

Justin didn't respond, but shot Kiami an accusing glance before he continued onward.

She had to duck to miss the ceiling as she followed them deeper into the rectangular vault. The burial place seemed to stretch out forever on either side of them.

Amanda turned to face them. "Let's separate to look. I don't know how the magic works. I found my missing stone when I was standing still. If you see anything odd, say something."

She stepped closer to Kiami and placed a hand on her shoulder. "Be patient in your search."

Kiami had nodded back before Amanda had walked away down the corridor, but she wasn't sure where Amanda expected her to look. There wasn't much here that she could see beyond a few shelves that held canisters and jars. After a quick inspection of those, she moved on.

Justin and Emily busied themselves searching the area around the few coffin-shaped blocks, whereas Amanda seemed to be walking the length of the wall. She would pause every few steps to look up to the ceiling and then back to the ground before moving on a few more paces. Kiami turned around in a circle, hoping maybe she would feel something.

She had to assume that the others' individual search efforts wouldn't yield any results, at least not in recovering her own missing gemstone. From what Amanda had told them of the tomb, only she would be able to find it.

She would have to go with her gut. She took a furtive step forward and then dropped down into a kneeling position on the sand-colored floor. She had experienced an urge to do so when she first entered the cave, but it had seemed silly. Now, as she began to crawl forward on her hands and knees, it felt right, although she did hope that no one was watching her too closely.

Her eyes lit when she saw a glint in the sand. She tried not to get her hopes up as she snagged something on her finger. She wondered if it could really be that easy as she pushed the dirt aside and dug deeper.

She pulled at the familiar chain, holding her breath as she did. She didn't let it out until she saw the moonstone dangling before her eyes. She hesitated as she lifted it up to place it around her neck. But as she debated whether it was a good idea to adorn herself with the gem or not, Amanda approached her. "We won't let it happen again unless you want it to."

Kiami knew that she was of course referring to the boy on the beach and the thing Amanda had witnessed. "How?"

"We will figure it out. You said it yourself. We have to take it one thing at a time."

Kiami placed the necklace around her neck and Amanda added, "It really is a lovely jewel."

Justin looked relieved when they exited the tomb. Happy, she supposed, that they hadn't encountered any of those giant spiders Amanda had mentioned.

She almost regretted what she needed to do before they left to search for Bloise. But now that she was reunited with her stone, she was even more certain that she needed to tell Emily and Amanda about the day his parents died. Maybe, she thought, there would be something in the story that would help them all. She chewed at one of her nails; he wasn't going to be happy with her.

She approached him, reaching for his arm and giving it a gentle squeeze. "You have to tell them the story."

In an instant, his eyes hardened, and he stepped back away from her. "No."

Kiami placed her hands on her hips. "If you don't, I will."

Both Amanda and Emily had turned to stare at them. "Are you going to let her boss me around like that?"

Amanda offered him only a sheepish grin in response as Emily said, "Whatever you are holding back, now is the time."

Justin looked down at his feet. "It feels like you guys are ganging up on me." He turned to glare back at Kiami. "Why now?"

"It could be important, Justin. I gave you time to think about it. Who knows how long we have before the jinn expect us to have this whole thing solved?" She crossed her arms over her chest. "And what if they don't come back to offer us any more guidance?"

His face scrunched up, and he turned away for a moment. When he turned back, his eyes glistened with emotion.

He gave a hurried retelling of the tale, looking up at her and scowling several times during the reiteration. She thought that he hit all the key points, so she was satisfied with what she had done.

A few excruciating moments of silence followed his story before Amanda spoke. "It sounds to me like when the accident happened, you went to another realm. It's a place I have been. Dangerous, though. Time moves really fast there. I think it is where the beings of pure energy live..." She trailed off thoughtfully.

Justin stomped his foot in her direction. "It's not true! I can't travel through the realms."

Amanda shrugged. "Maybe you couldn't then. Perhaps it was your father. Only you haven't attempted it since you have held your emerald," she coaxed.

"It would be helpful," Kiami added, nodding. A bleak look settled onto his face, and she knew he was still thinking of the accident. She reached out and placed a reassuring hand on his shoulder, but he pulled away from her.

"I can't. I won't try," he said stubbornly, kicking at the dirt with his foot and pushing the hair back from his forehead.

"But Justin," Emily started to say, but she was cut off by an outburst from Amanda.

"Fine! Damn the consequences!"

She could see the outrage in Amanda's eyes as she lifted her staff and called to her magic in a fit of anger. Kiami wished that Amanda wouldn't have been so impatient, but it seemed Justin really knew how to push her buttons. She hoped their mistrust of each other wasn't as permanent as it seemed.

## ENDOW

The shadow magic swirled out of the staff, engulfing them as Amanda used the gem to travel again.

# 25

## Emily - Bloise

Emily was relieved when she saw that they had arrived at a place that looked much like Amanda, Kiami, and Justin had described it. She didn't want any more surprises today.

She tried to shake off the uneasiness that followed each of their trips as she took in her surroundings. Sand dunes stretched out in all directions. To Emily, this place looked harsh and desolate. The sun's rays were unrelenting.

She crinkled her sweaty forehead in dismay as Amanda revealed what was in the satchel she had brought along. From inside the bag, she had pulled out four coarse hooded cloaks and asked them to pull them on over their clothing. They had only just arrived, and she was already damp with perspiration. Even after Kiami and Justin had donned theirs, she held hers out in front of her as if she was inspecting it.

Amanda must have noticed her unwillingness to comply, because she said, "I don't know all the rules here, Em, but I do know that when we walked through the market to the palace, Erol covered himself in a cloak like these, and I was made to as well. Also," she added as she turned to Justin, "they don't like jinn much, or so I was told anyway. So please do not reveal yourself. At least not until we are inside the palace."

Emily thought that Justin seemed a little irritated by her announcement. Of course, he had already been upset with them all before they traveled.

"I do know that Bloise isn't really one of them... you know, an arcane." She added, "But I'm not sure of the old wizard's background. When I was here last, he was controlling the ruler, using magic." A serious look was pasted on her face. "The wizard, Bloise, just likes the ruler to believe he is still in charge. Be wary of him."

Even though it felt somewhat inappropriate, Emily couldn't help but smile. She cherished the thought of escaping this vast brown desert. She longed for cover from the sun and an escape from the sand that seemed to creep up under the layers of her garments. It was hard for her to imagine people lived in this environment.

As Amanda escorted them through the sand, the robe weighed Emily down. She soon became tired. The farther she trudged upward, the more her leg muscles ached.

She was planning to ask for a break at the top of the dune they had just ascended when Amanda thrust a water bottle out in front of her, and she accepted it, drinking in big gulps. It wasn't cold, but it gave her a much-needed energy boost.

"You will make yourself sick, Em," Kiami warned.

She handed the bottle back, wiping her mouth on her sleeve as she did, and Amanda pointed down the other side of the dune. "Not much farther."

Emily's heart leapt at the sight ahead. A short way in the distance stood several white rectangular buildings protruding up out of the sand and blocking some of the sun's harsh rays.

As they got closer, she saw encrusted paths full of people dressed in heavy robes like their own, many with tan- and copper-colored horses accompanying them.

In the center rose a massive square structure with a domed top. "Is that the palace?"

"Yes," Amanda whispered. "Stay close."

What appeared to be a busy market area lay between them and their destination. Emily followed so close behind Amanda that she stepped on her robe on more than one occasion, causing her to stop and glance back at Emily with a disapproving glare.

Several merchants beckoned to them as they passed by their stalls, offering trinkets, food, or clothing. But Amanda would only shake her head in response before moving on.

As hot as she was, Emily would have liked to check out their wares. She reminded herself that Amanda had said such interactions would be dangerous especially for Justin, so Emily mirrored her actions and kept her head down.

When they finally made it through the crowd of shoppers, Emily threw a pitiful glance back in the direction of the market, wishing she could have looked around more.

Muscular men with leathery, weather-worn skin lined the palace entrance. But Amanda didn't approach right away. Instead, she moved her head from side to side in slow motion as if she was looking for someone in particular. Clad in identical white clothing, from this distance, the guards all looked very similar.

She addressed Kiami and Emily. "You two stay back here until I signal to you. Justin comes with me."

Emily watched as she approached one of the guards. This one had a jagged scar that started at the base of his chin and ended just below his eye.

Emily was horrified when she saw Amanda remove Justin's hood, and she tried to rush forward, only to find that Kiami had a tight grip on her robe. "Amanda said to stay put." There was a sternness in her voice that Emily hadn't heard often.

She gasped in exasperation. "But what is she doing? Using him for bait?"

"I don't know, but whatever she did, it worked. Come on."

Emily turned to see that Amanda was beckoning them ahead, and to her relief, Justin was moving forward of his own accord.

She followed Kiami up the steps to the entrance and through the doors. Once they were inside, Amanda pushed her hood back, so Emily did the same.

She walked softly so that her shoes would not make noise as she moved across the shining marble floor.

They entered a spectacular hall with ceilings at least twenty feet high. In the center of the room was a massive black brazier, brimming with burning, crackling flames.

Vases adorned with intricate designs lined the walls, and Emily had to stop herself from reaching out to run her fingers over the tiny hand-painted images that covered them as she passed by.

On the other side of the room was an impressive throne studded with gems and rubies. The golden-hued seat was empty, but echoes of music could be heard from another room in the distance.

The music became louder as they were pushed onward into another grand room. This one had a fountain about as tall as she was at its center.

Instead of the water cascading down around the tiers and into the basin, it remained suspended, as if it was frozen in place.

She reached out and touched one of the suspended droplets, pulling back her hand as her fingers became wet. It wasn't frozen, just hovering there. An unfamiliar voice broke the silence as she examined it. "It's a consequence, I suspect." Emily looked up at the white-haired wizard. Crow's feet radiated from the corners of his eyes, and dimples appeared on his cheeks as he grinned at her. He was covered in a silvery robe that shimmered as he moved closer. This, she thought, had to be Bloise.

"The water just simply stopped moving some hours ago. I doubt many have noticed, apart from me. They are much too busy celebrating."

Emily lifted her eyebrows. "What are they celebrating?" She could see what looked like dozens of people in the next room moving in a rhythmic dance.

"Our ruler has decided to step down. He has come to doubt his own sanity, you see. So many strange things happening." He winked at her before turning to address Amanda. "Your friends should come in and meet him."

Amanda gave a slight curtsy as she answered, "If you insist, wizard."

She must have assumed introductions were not warranted, Emily thought. The wizard looked at her again and smiled before turning his back to her and moving ahead into the crowded room.

Amanda laid her satchel at the edge of the fountain. "Take your cloaks off." She lifted hers up and over her head to reveal a sparkling black dress that reached her ankles.

Emily opened her mouth in surprise at the wardrobe change.

Amanda's eyes danced as she glanced at her. "It's a trick, an illusion. Hurry up."

"But is Justin safe?"

Amanda shrugged back at her. "Erol was after we talked to Bloise."

"That was Bloise then, I presume?" She nodded and signaled for them to follow as she worked her way through the jovial guests.

Emily pulled the hooded cloak over her head to reveal a light purple gown that looked identical to the one Amanda had on. She shoved her cloak into the satchel and hurried to catch up. Justin and Kiami had already moved ahead without her.

The fast tempo had relaxed to a steady beat. The attendees had slowed their movements and were now dancing in graceful, smooth circles around the room.

The wizard and Amanda had stopped in front of a large, sequined pillow.

As Emily approached, she could see that the man sitting upon it appeared exhausted. His eyes were wide, with a glazed look, and remained unblinking below his single bushy eyebrow.

He stared back, expressionless, as Bloise bowed and gestured in their direction. "You remember Amanda, sir."

The ruler nodded, but his face didn't change. Emily doubted he knew what was going on at all.

Bloise moved his hand in her direction, then made a sweeping motion toward the others. "Emily, Justin, and Kiami." She wondered how he knew their names and guessed that Amanda must have told him before she made it to this side of the room.

She snuck a glimpse in Justin's direction. He was now wearing long pants and an uncomfortable-looking tunic. Kiami stood next to him, and she could see that the dress she had on was designed like her own, except that it was made of a thin white material. It looked similar to what she normally wore.

The ruler pushed himself up to stand, and to her wonderment, she could see that every inch of his exposed skin was adorned with brightly colored tattoos.

"Maybe you would care for a dance with the ladies?" Bloise smirked and lifted his eyebrows.

Amanda raised her hand in objection. "We don't have time for this."

"Nonsense," he said, dropping his smile.

She had a feeling what he really meant was closer to *"You will do as I say or go away."*

The ruler thrust a hand in her direction, and Emily took a step back. Bloise moved behind her and placed a hand on her shoulder as he leaned close to her ear. "Don't disappoint him, my dear."

Emily was not much of a dancer, and her heart pounded in her chest as the ruler took hold of her waist, pulling her into the sea of people.

He moved across the crowded dance floor in a robotic fashion. He never flinched or uttered a word, even though she stepped on his feet several times while she attempted to follow his lead.

She couldn't seem to relax, and her movements remained just as stiff as his own throughout the song. She was relieved when he guided her back over to Amanda and the others.

Bloise reached out and took Kiami's fingers in his hand, pulling her toward the ruler. "I think you will find Kiami a much more graceful dance partner."

As he placed her hand in the ruler's, he added, "Maybe she will even end the dance with a kiss?" The smile melted off Kiami's face, and Bloise winked back at her.

Amanda shook her head at Bloise, and Kiami moved onto the dance floor with her partner. Somehow, with Kiami in his arms, his movements seemed much more fluid. She put her hands on her hips. "Is this really necessary?"

Bloise glanced in her direction. "All's fair in times of war, my dear."

*A war? Is that what this is?* Emily wondered.

"You will say just about anything to get a rise out of someone, won't you?" Amanda scolded.

"No, but I'm having a good time. Do you remember what having fun is like, Amanda? If you are bored, maybe I could draw some attention to

Justin's heritage. That should raise a commotion."

"Don't lie, Bloise. Apart from the poor ruler, this isn't any more real than the clothes we appear to have on."

"Ah, you learned some things in the time since you were here last."

Amanda nodded, folding her arms over her chest. "More than I ever wanted to."

Up until this point, Amanda had kept her interactions with Bloise so cordial that Emily was a bit surprised by the outburst, more so by the fact that this shindig was fake. It all seemed very real to her.

She watched the guests for a few minutes before it struck her. She realized that although she could see, hear, and feel them, the smell was off. A sweet aroma wafted through the room instead of the scent of sweat and vigor that you would expect.

She peered over her shoulder at Justin's face. By the look of astonishment in his features, she could see that he had been just as shocked by the news.

The song changed several times before Kiami returned. When she did, Bloise motioned to Amanda. "Take them to my quarters. I trust that you remember the way?"

She nodded. "I can manage."

Amanda led them down several flights of stairs and waved them through some brightly colored curtains. As Emily passed into the room she saw that similar cloths were draped over every wall in Bloise's living quarters.

The room was very sparsely furnished. Emily assumed that the myriad large pillows placed around the floor at random were meant for sitting on.

Other than those, there was only a spacious wardrobe and a large round bed positioned near each other on one side of the room.

Amanda caught her eyes as she cautioned them, "Don't say too much." Then she placed her finger over her lips to hush them before they could respond.

Bloise entered, followed by six smiling women dressed in brightly colored, sheer fabrics. Emily hadn't missed the way Amanda scowled at them as they walked past her. "No wardrobe changes or piercings. Dismiss them."

The outfits did leave little to the imagination, Emily thought as she looked away, trying to avoid eye contact with them.

"Oh, relax," Bloise said. "Are you still afraid of needles?"

This drew Emily's attention back in Bloise's direction, and he winked at her. Amanda crossed her arms over her chest. "There is no need for these theatrics."

"There's always a need for theatrics, dear." His eyes danced with excitement. "But have it your way." He spoke a few words in a strange tongue, and the ladies turned and made a slow escape.

After they exited the room, he walked over to Kiami and lifted her chin with his index finger. "The ability to control others with song." He stepped away from her and turned back to face Amanda. "That is what you want to know about, yes?"

"That's part of it," Amanda responded.

"Nasty business, borrowing magical abilities. I shouldn't have done it

I vowed not to do such things again, but sometimes the temptation is just too strong." He smiled slyly. "It's how I ended up here, you know, pretending to work for that dimwit upstairs."

Emily felt like that was an invitation to ask questions, but Amanda had warned them to be careful what they said to Bloise, and she didn't want to take the chance.

He turned back to face Kiami. "I would love to see you demonstrate it for me; it's been a while."

Kiami looked down at her feet. "I would rather not."

He shrugged. "Fine. The magic, it came from the realm of the goddesses. Terrible shame that they haven't been back there in a long while." He raised his eyebrows and looked around the room before continuing. "Something they created for their own descendants, I would guess."

When Kiami didn't answer, he added, "Now, what other question do I see dancing on your lips?"

Amanda pushed her way in between them. "First, tell us what you want from us."

Bloise stepped back and rubbed at his arm where she had pushed him. "You don't have to be so feisty. My old bones are sensitive. What makes you think I want something?"

Amanda cocked her head to the side with a knowing smile. "You and I both know that you don't give away help or information for free."

He nodded and eyed her up and down. "You were a quick study from the beginning. Jacob should have been more careful."

Amanda glowered at him.

"He's still around, you know. Just because you took his magic and scrambled him up a bit doesn't mean he has forgotten everything."

When Amanda had told them Etzion's tale of the man in the woods, she had mentioned that his description made her think of the sorcerer who had once held her captive. *Could it be the same person?* Emily wondered.

Amanda had said she didn't believe it was possible after so many years.

*If she didn't believe it, why did she bother to mention it at all?* she wondered.

Emily felt goosebumps prickle on the back of her neck as Bloise walked a slow circle around them, rubbing at his chin as if he was evaluating them. He stopped again, close to Amanda. "Back when we first met, I told you that I planned on being prepared for whatever nastiness is coming." He stared hard at her, and she nodded. "Something far worse than that old sorcerer is here, and well, thus far I have only managed to get by, so I can't take no for an answer. You all understand?"

Emily nodded and glanced at the others. Justin and Kiami both agreed, but Amanda stood firm and unmoving. "You may have them fooled, but I will not agree to something if I don't know what it is."

"What I want is nothing more than a trinket, really, one from each of you. And I promise to give you more than just the information Kiami seeks."

Amanda pasted a smile on her face. "What kind of information is that?"

"I know many things, valuable things. I know that the world is changing, that the realms are faltering, that things are leaking in. I know what Kiami saw on the other side of the bridge, and I know why it's significant. I also know where you can find the puppeteer that has orchestrated all you have endured."

Amanda's smirk disappeared, and Emily could see anger dancing behind her eyes as she squeezed one hand into a tight fist.

Bloise raised a finger to signal that he wasn't finished. "But after I have answered Kiami's question, I will only answer one more. You will have to decide what is most important. There are eyes watching always, and I have already put myself at risk just giving you an audience. If I didn't need those trinkets, I wouldn't have taken the chance at all."

Amanda nodded. Her face had turned a shade of red.

Bloise gave one quick nod. "Good. The changes have already started, things have been seen by humans. Things that can't be unseen... a bandage won't fix what's broken. And you, this whole motley entourage, is only a bandage. You will have to find what's missing before the true battle begins. Now, enough dilly-dallying. What I need is a drop of Amanda's blood, a lock of Emily's hair, a feather from Kiami, and for Justin to light a candle for me." He snapped his fingers on one hand and a silver lantern appeared within it. He handed it to Justin and then snapped his fingers again, revealing a small pocketknife.

Emily accepted the blade, knowing she was meant to cut a lock of her hair with it.

Bloise turned toward the entrance. "I will leave you alone for a few minutes while you each do what you need to do."

With Bloise's exit, Justin erupted with questions aimed at Amanda. "You said not to trust him, yet we are going to give him what he wants?"

"I told you that there would have to be a bargain."

"How do we know what he's going to do with this stuff?"

"We don't. But it's a game we have to play. Unless you see an alternative?"

"We can trick him, make him think we gave him what he wanted. Can't you use a spell similar to the one you used earlier?"

Amanda shook her head. "He would know if we try to deceive him in that way."

Justin pushed his hair back from his face. "I don't like it."

"Neither do I," Kiami added, "but I want my mom's journal. Maybe it can confirm what he said."

"What about the other question? The one he offered to answer?" Emily added.

Amanda said, "That's easy. We want to know who the puppeteer is."

Justin stood up taller and puffed out his chest. "No. *You* want to know."

Kiami placed a hand on her hip. "They all seem like important questions."

Amanda looked Emily in the eyes and asked, "What do you think, Emily?"

They all turned to her, and her stomach knotted. "I–I... agree with Amanda," she blurted. She wasn't really sure what she thought, but she had panicked.

"That's settled then. Justin, light the lantern," Amanda ordered.

He looked upset, but didn't seem to want to argue. He opened the small door that allowed access to the wick and lit the flame.

Emily noticed it was much easier for him now than it had been on the day at the pond.

As he closed the door and latched it, three small compartments slid open from the side of the base. They looked like little drawers.

"I think we are meant to put the other trinkets in these," Amanda said, pointing at one of them.

"Seems so," Emily said as she flipped open the pocketknife and reached for one of her purple curls. She wrapped the strand around her finger until it pulled at her scalp and raised the knife up, slicing through with little effort. She just wanted this whole thing to be over with. She placed the small lock into one of the compartment drawers, and it slid closed.

Emily turned to Amanda and handed her the open blade. "Do you need help?"

Amanda shook her head and grabbed the handle. Emily watched as she carefully poked at the end of her finger until a pearl of red blood formed there. Amanda flipped the blade closed and leaned down, sliding it into the top of her heeled boot.

Emily averted her eyes, training them on the lantern, pretending that she hadn't noticed the theft.

Amanda reached over to one of the open compartments of the lantern with her damaged hand and squeezed the end of her finger until the droplet fell in. As the compartment slid closed, Emily turned to Kiami.

"Ready?"

Kiami shook her head. "Are we sure that it's worth it? I mean…"

Amanda interrupted, "Kiami, we already made a deal."

"Fine." Kiami changed quickly, and Amanda bent forward over her, plucking a small feather from her backside.

She waited for Kiami to change back before handing it to her. "I think you should put it in there yourself."

Kiami snatched the small feather from her hand and placed it in the last compartment. As it slid closed, Bloise called through the curtain, "Are you about finished?"

"Yes," Amanda responded.

He pushed his way through the barrier and walked straight to the lantern. When he picked it up, he turned it in his hand, as if he was inspecting its primitive design. "Good. Very good." He snapped the fingers on his free hand, and the lantern disappeared. "Now," he said, turning to Kiami.

"First, let me ask, what do you know about this journal that you seek in the first place?"

"Not a lot. I never had a chance to read it." Amanda shot her a look, and Emily realized Kiami had said more than she wanted her to.

Bloise lifted a book in his hand and started to thumb through the pages. "I am afraid you will find more questions than answers in here. However," he added, "I can offer some advice.

"Don't follow Amanda where she is going. The rest of you will only find temptations there. I don't think you four have the same, hm, resistance that she does. Instead, find the others."

"Others?" Amanda asked, pretending to be oblivious.

"Well, yes, I thought it was obvious by now. Aeron, as you called him, wasn't lying that there are seven of you. One descendant from each species, or a better term, one half-blood for each realm. Now, the real question is, how will you proceed to find the rest?"

"You let us worry about that," Amanda responded. Emily wondered how Bloise knew what questions they would ask before they even had a chance to say them. She doubted Amanda would offer her any insight if she interrogated her later.

"Fine with me. But just remember, it was not an accident that you four were brought together. Think about what led you forward to begin with."

Amanda shifted beside her uneasily as Justin took a step closer to Bloise. "The gems? Is that what you're really after?"

"They are very powerful sources of energy, indeed. But I know very little of them." Bloise smiled and shook his head. "I am sure you have noticed that those gemstones can only be handled by certain individuals. I lack the proper lineage, dear boy."

Emily knew he was telling the truth; she had seen it with her own eyes when the small boy burned his hand on her amethyst.

Bloise's eyes danced with merriment as he pointed at Justin. "This one doesn't believe, even with all the evidence piling up. I wish I could just pretend it wasn't true myself. But hey, there can be value in stubbornness. At the right time, it will be a benefit to the rest of you, mark my words."

Emily noticed that Amanda relaxed her shoulders a bit at his prediction.

Bloise then spun toward Kiami. "Now, can I have that journal for a second?

Kiami seemed reluctant to give the book back, and Bloise shot her a knowing smile as she handed it over.

"All in good time, dear. You won't need it where you're going right now."

Emily thought that a strange remark, but odder still was that he seemed to flip the book open to a random page, and yet it appeared to be exactly the one he wanted. He lifted the book for them to get a better view.

"There, see this?" He pointed to an illustration. "The mountain range here, this is where your answers lie. There are things there you need to find out, but there are also things there that have the capability of destroying you all. I do hope that you take my advice, Amanda. Leave them behind when you seek the puppeteer."

His smile faltered as he looked around the room. "The real battle hasn't started yet, and in order for all of you to be prepared to fight like the gods and monsters you are, she must do this alone."

The grin returned to his lips as he closed the book and handed it back to Kiami. He grabbed her hand as she reached for it and whispered loud enough for Emily to hear, "Have you ever thought to ask her how she knew where your necklace was?"

Kiami squirmed out of his grip. "She had been there before. And," she added in a stern voice, "I could ask you the same question about all of this."

He scratched at his chin. "Hmm, I suppose you are right, but if I were you, I would ask Amanda harder questions."

Kiami barked, "I think you only tell the truth when it suits you."

Emily glanced over at Amanda. She seemed a bit irritated by the encounter, but she made no move to interfere. Emily hoped Bloise would grow tired of this game soon. He already had what he wanted, so she didn't understand why he kept it up.

He rubbed his hands together as he turned to address Amanda. "Now, how are you planning to get back to the human realm?"

# 26

# Amanda - Hara Berezaiti

When Bloise offered to create a portal to send them back to the human realm, Amanda was happy to accept. The feat, he explained, was much easier to accomplish since the barriers were weaker.

She was sure there was more to it than that. The possibility that he was using his new trinkets to boost his own abilities crossed her mind, but she wasn't going to bring it up then and have the others fret over it. Especially since she had insisted it was the only way.

She didn't want to use her stone again unless she had to, and she had been finding it difficult to control her anger as it was. She hadn't missed his attempts to raise doubts about her in the others in order to provoke her.

She breathed slowly in and out, willing her heart to stop racing. He had been whispering things to Kiami. Truths she wasn't willing to face right now.

She stood looking in the mirror in Emily's bathroom with her hands wrapped around the edge of the sink.

"One thing at a time."

She took a few slower breaths and then let go of the sink before pushing her hair back out of her face. She was going to find that puppeteer.

She smiled at her reflection. She had definitely made an improvement on holding her tongue and her temper.

Amanda had never been comfortable with the idea of walking through the town to begin with, and now, as she poked around the bookstore, she couldn't help but feel like someone was watching her.

She had gone off by herself to try to find the location of the mountain range, and now she wished that she had asked Kiami or Emily to join her.

Amanda peered out the window. From here, she had a clear view of the stone monument in the center of the park.

Bloise's statements about Jacob certainly hadn't helped. She wondered if there had been any truth behind his words when he insinuated he could be wandering close by, or if he had only mentioned it to annoy her.

Goosebumps rose on her arms, and she rubbed them away as she whispered to herself, "I don't know what's worse: a town full of jinn that you can't trust or a completely empty one. It's just all-around creepy."

The townspeople were still nowhere to be seen, and the door to the lower level of the bookstore remained invisible, just as Emily had told her.

Amanda glanced at the pile of books she had been stacking on the counter. She thought about hefting them into her arms and rushing out the door, although she had intended on remaining in the bookshop while she researched the mountain range from the illustration. She didn't want the others to know exactly where she was going.

She opened the door and walked out onto the street, aligning herself with the window. She took a few steps forward and looked around before moving on into the town square. From her new vantage point, she could see that the stores on this side of the street had been covered or had shutters closed over them to lessen the damage of the storm.

She looked down at the green blanket of grass beneath her feet and then up at the stone-carved tree. She remembered the statue from her vision of Emily. She reached out and placed a hand against the surface of its trunk.

The stone was cold to the touch, and several runes that she recognized were carved low at its base. She had seen the same symbols before on the tree from the dream realm, and also in the forest with her father at the beginning of her journey. But this was not the natural tree-like those had been.

She reached up and touched her own runic scars. Hers had been carved there by Jacob during her imprisonment to aid in her movement through the realms. She wondered what purpose they could serve on a stone tree. She was certain it couldn't be used for travel; it had no real roots, after all, and she had learned that it was the roots of the trees that had really connected them to the other realms.

Amanda slowly circled the tree, staring up at the clumsily carved branches. As she moved to dunk below one of the lower limbs, she thought she caught a slight movement from the corner of her eye.

She ran her hands over the branch at a slow and steady pace, feeling for any difference in the texture or temperature. When she reached one of the knuckles that had been carved into the jointed branch, she lifted her hand for a moment.

As she had run her hands along the surface, she noticed that the stone seemed a tiny bit warmer near the bulging knuckles, and the stone didn't seem so firm. She smacked her hand down on the spot and thought she felt something quiver below the surface.

The covering of the knuckles on this branch was not solid. The area seemed to be more like a thin membrane. Since she had left her staff behind so that she wouldn't be tempted to use it, her only physical weapon was the pocketknife she had taken when they visited Bloise.

Amanda bent down to retrieve the small blade from her boot and flicked it open. If she was wrong, the knife would not be able to penetrate the surface.

She raised her arm and brought the sharp knife down with as much force as she could. As it disappeared into the tree's protruding knuckle, a clear liquid began to seep from the hole. Her heart leapt in her chest as she pulled the knife free.

A knuckle on the same branch had vanished, and in its place, a large round eye stared back at her. It was not an intelligent eye, like the ones that occurred naturally in the center of the flowers she had encountered in the Chaos realm.

This eye held no emotion, no recognition of what was happening. It was a tool, she assumed, added to the statue by an outside force. It occurred to her again that Abaddon had said he was watching the jinn town. Perhaps it hadn't been him at all, but rather the person that had sent him to find her to begin with.

Amanda's face felt hot as she lifted the blade again, this time directing it at the open eye farther down the length of the branch. It never flinched as she moved the knife toward its center, stabbing at the pupil. The same clear liquid began to ooze out, and the membrane reappeared, covering the socket.

She stood still for a moment, eyeing the branch, unsure if her blade had really caused any damage to the magical growths. She reached up and placed her hand over one of the knuckles. It now felt much harder and colder to the touch, as if it had returned to its stone state. Amanda studied the other branches, testing a few knots that were within her reach with the tip of her blade, but they had all solidified. Whoever had been spying had retreated, at least for now.

She replaced the knife and made her way back into the bookstore, wondering if this was one of the things Bloise had attempted to warn her of, in his roundabout way. He hadn't been the first to speak of eyes watching. When she had captured Jacqueline, one of the odd riddles she told Amanda had to do with eyes and roots. She scowled as she tried to push the invading memory away. She had research to do.

Hara Berezaiti was the mountain she was looking for; she was sure of it. The pictures were the best match to the one she had seen in the sketch, and she had pored over the other images for hours. None looked quite the same to her.

She had been careful to replace the books before she left, but the haphazard way that they were displayed in the store made it hard for her to remember the exact locations she had found them in.

Even though the feeling of being watched had not returned, she glanced over at the tree statue on her way out of the bookstore, wondering how long it would be before the spying eyes reappeared.

When she reached the house where Emily had been boarding, she grabbed her satchel and began stuffing it full of essentials, starting with granola bars and water.

If she wanted to avoid using her gemstone, she would have to hike at least part of the way up the mountain. She could travel for a distance with the use of her shadow magic alone, but she doubted it would take her all the way without the assistance of control that the black diamond provided to her.

Since she used to hike with her father on a regular basis, there were a few more principal things that she wouldn't have wanted to start her journey without. She searched the house's cabinets and cupboards, foraging for matches, first-aid supplies, and a flashlight.

She was rummaging around in the coat closet when Justin startled her. "What are you doing?"

Amanda didn't bother to turn around as she placed a hat aside and continued her search. "Looking for something warmer, gloves, a coat. I don't suppose your aunt would have a compass somewhere?"

"But why?"

"I think I have found the mountain range; I'm leaving."

"You're just going to run off realm-hopping by yourself after all that 'we work together' stuff? Figures."

"First off, it's here in the human realm. Second, I should go alone. You heard Bloise."

Amanda hadn't realized Kiami had been standing behind her with Justin until she spoke up. "Wait, Amanda. Look at this. The book pages are all blank now. It has to be a trap."

She turned around, her eyes darting over the journal that Kiami held up, and shrugged.

There was a chance that it could be a trap, but although Bloise always remained vague in his directions, he had not lied about anything so far.

There was a reason he had insisted she go alone, and she was sure it would be clear once she reached her destination.

"I don't think Bloise wants us dead, not yet, at least. Does he have ulterior motives? Possibly. I am not dragging you along with me either way."

"How will we find the others without you?" Kiami questioned.

"You guys wait for Etzion and then start the search for the others. He will be able to help you. Who knows, maybe we won't even need them."

"You don't believe that. Do you?" Kiami probed.

She didn't, but decided to skirt the question. "Sometimes you get an itch that you have to scratch no matter what."

"Then let me come with you," Kiami pleaded,

"I am going, and you are staying."

Amanda shifted her gaze to Justin. "Something is using the stone tree in the center of town to keep an eye on things, and I don't believe it's the jinn. I think I stopped it for now, but will you look into it?"

"Is it that Jacob guy?"

Amanda shook her head. "No. It can't be. Even if he somehow managed to get through the barrier to town, there is no way for him to get his magic back."

He crossed his arms over his chest and gave a silent nod before Amanda turned away with a jerk. She stuffed the items she had found into her bag and pushed past them. "Do not try to follow me, Kiami, or you will be sorry."

# 27

# Kiami - Going Hunting

Kiami had recognized the mountain from the first moment Bloise showed it to the others. Hara Berezaiti was one of the many places her mother and Jacqueline had told her about when teaching her myths. Stories revered the mountain as a watch post for the sky. In fact, it was said that all the stars revolved around that particular peak.

She remembered the story well because she had thought Hara Berezaiti was an odd choice for a watch post when there were so many wider and taller mountains on the planet.

"It may not be the biggest," her mom had laughed, "but it's hardly the smallest." And then she had looked at her with such seriousness in her eyes that Kiami had found herself unable to look away. "As for why the stars would have chosen to revolve around that particular summit, you must remember that what makes something special is not always visible."

She had mulled over the memory for hours after they returned to Emily's. She wanted to be optimistic, but she was sure that between her mother's words and the expression on her face, it had been some kind of warning.

She had only just worked up the courage to explain this to Amanda when she realized that all of the pages in the book had gone blank, and now she was gone.

Kiami had grabbed a cloak from the closet and turned to follow Amanda out the door, but Justin grabbed at her forearm. "Don't go. You heard what she said."

"Get your hand off of me."

"If she is using her magic, she will be long gone already anyway."

Kiami closed her eyes as she shook her head. She knew that the mountain was very far away, and without the aid of Amanda's black diamond, she wouldn't be able to make the whole journey at once.

"If she is trying to avoid using her gemstone, she will need to make part of the journey on foot. I can catch up."

"And if she decided to use it, what then?"

"I know where she is going!" She yanked her arm lose with such force that he tottered forward, landing hard on one knee. "I am sick of you trying to tell me what to do and not to do. If she veers off track, I will hunt her down. I have a natural talent for things like that." Guilt at causing him to fall rained down on her even as she spoke, but she refused to allow it to change her mind.

He grimaced as he spat out his next words. "She doesn't want you to go. She does not want our help with this."

Kiami backed out the door, almost tripping herself up on the frame. "Stop being so stubborn. Tell Emily that I will be back."

She looked for any sign of Amanda, but it appeared Justin had been right. Amanda had used her magic to leave as fast as possible. But Kiami's conversation with him had given her an idea, and although she did recognize the mountains in the picture, she wondered if it was possible to track magic. If it was, now would be the perfect time to find evidence of it.

For a moment, she thought about running back into the house to retrieve her hidden necklace. After they returned from Bloise's, she had tucked it away for safekeeping to prevent herself from using it.

She looked at the house and chewed at her nail. *No*, she thought as she pulled her fingertips away, *if I bring it with me, I will end up using it.*

Her transformation into an owl was almost immediate. In this form, she had always been excellent at hunting and chasing, but she had always sought animals. Recognizing and following magic was a new concept she had never explored.

She glided in a large circle around the property, trying to detect anything off: a sound, a smell, the slightest hint of movement.

She passed over a section of the property that emanated with the light buzz of electricity, so faint she almost missed it. It elevated into the air from a very small area in the yard.

As she swooped in close, she investigated the space, scrutinizing the smallest details, things she knew a human wouldn't be able to detect.

Sure enough, on closer inspection, she found that a tiny amount of fading dark tendrils hung in the air like a shadowy residue.

Even though she realized the signs she found would fade fast, she was still excited at the possibilities of use for her newfound knowledge, but before she could tell Emily or Justin, she would need to catch up with Amanda and warn her away from the mountain.

She flew northward as fast as she could, even though she knew her wings would never come close to moving her as fast as Amanda's shadow magic.

# 28

# Emily - Of Talismans and Tales

The force of the door slamming echoed throughout the house, rousing Emily from her thoughts. The beginning of the day had been rather quiet and uneventful, with everyone seeming to be keeping to themselves.

She hadn't thought to question it, not until she heard the bang of wood against wood. From the way the noise cracked into the air, she thought the door should have come off its hinges on impact.

Emily made her way to the window and peered out. She suppressed the urge to push it open and call to Justin as she watched him stomp off.

Instead, she moved to her bedroom door, shouting out Kiami and Amanda's names as she swung it open. When no one answered her, she walked through the hall, peeking into the other rooms as she passed by.

The way Justin had stormed off, she thought, it appeared that he was blowing off steam. As she looked for them, she wondered what had made him so angry. When she made her way to the lower level, it became apparent that the house was empty.

Emily chewed at her bottom lip, questioning why both Kiami and Amanda would leave without bothering to say anything. She placed a hand on her hip and glanced around the unoccupied space, as if a clue would pop out at her.

She knew that if Justin had been chasing after them, he wouldn't have remained in human form. He would have used his jinn abilities to move faster.

She let out a sigh and then made her way out the front door. She didn't want to wait around to find out what had happened.

Justin had been moving toward the main area of town, so she would walk in that direction. She knew there was a good chance she would come across him without much effort, unless he was hiding from her. The town wasn't that big.

She spotted Justin as she approached the town square. He seemed to be hard at work hanging disk-like objects on the stone tree at its center.

He was concentrating so hard on the task that he didn't even seem to notice her approach. When he hung the last one, he made his way to the green bench and scooped up several more.

The orange disks stood out against the worn green of the paint on the benches, and she moved toward it, eyeing the pile of ornaments. There had to be several dozen.

Emily reached down and picked one up. On closer inspection, the palm-sized disk seemed almost more pink than orange.

The material felt rough against her skin as she flipped it around. A small hole had been made at the top to loop a chain or string through, and both sides were covered in tiny images.

"What are you doing?"

She placed the disk back in the pile. "I am wondering why you are decorating this tree with some kind of talisman."

"Amulet," he corrected as he moved closer and reached down to grab a few more. "A talisman is usually used to attract good fortune, and in general an amulet wards off or protects against evil."

Emily's face tightened with concern. "What happened?"

"Amanda said something before she left. She thinks that someone is using the tree to spy."

"But she said Abaddon was dead," she gulped as guilt began to gnaw at her stomach. Amanda had told her what Abaddon said, and she had brushed it aside as unimportant.

"I am not sure what happened while she was here. She didn't go into detail. What do you know about it?"

Emily shrugged and looked away. "She said he told her that he couldn't manifest himself in town, but that he had an anchor in the center. A place where he could spy on the jinn villagers."

"Em, you should have mentioned this. I doubt it had been Abaddon doing the spying, and even if it was, someone else could have taken over."

"I'm sorry."

Justin pushed his hair back with his free hand. "Just help me tie these to the branches. There's some twine over by the tree."

She picked up another talisman. "Will these really help?"

"I hope so. Be sure not to miss any, even the smallest ones."

Emily focused on adding the talisman to the lower branches while Justin used his abilities to reach those highest up.

When they were finished, Justin came to her side as she stood looking up at the tree.

She had never noticed branches at the top were covered in long, sharp thorns. They looked as thick and strong as nails. She imagined they were a good deterrent for birds that were looking for a safe perch. If Justin had been in solid form, he couldn't have hung the talisman without coming into contact with them.

She glanced over at him. "It almost seemed like it would have been easier to get rid of the monument."

"This tree is more than a monument, Em." He reached for her hand, and she accepted it as he continued, "Let's not discuss this here. Just in case."

As they walked away from the square, Emily was reminded of why she had gone looking for him in town to begin with.

"Justin, you said before that Amanda left. Where did she go?"

"I should have gone to you as soon as they took off." He stopped and released her hand. "Please don't be upset, Emily."

"Kiami went with her?"

"More like chased after her. Amanda insisted on going alone."

Emily nodded. "She went to the place Bloise told her about. How did she find it?"

"I think she came to town to do research, and that's when she had an encounter with the tree."

Warmth rushed up her neck and into her cheeks. Emily folded her arms across her chest as she pulled her eyes away from his. "I just don't understand why you didn't come tell me."

"Because I was mad at them and worried, but I knew she wouldn't have said that about the tree unless something had happened. By the time I got there, I had cooled down, and as I looked up into its branches, I realized my own wrath has been getting in the way of our understanding."

She furrowed her brow as she shifted her gaze back up at him. "How so?" His straight-faced expression filled her with instant discomfort as his eyes penetrated hers.

"This mess that we are entangled in started way back with a myth that I wasn't privy to knowing. But the jinn did teach me things, like the history of this town. And I think it is directly linked to what we are going through."

She wished she hadn't asked. Even though no one was around to witness Justin pouring his heart out in the open, Emily felt exposed. Embarrassed at his sudden bout of honesty, she dropped her arms at her side and shifted her weight. "Let's get out of the street and back to the house."

"Wait. First, I need to apologize for the way I have been acting. The things I have done and said to Amanda, you, even Kiami. I have had no good cause to be so..."

"It's okay, Justin."

"No, it's not. Things started in wrath never turn out for the better."

Once they were back at Nina's, the tense seriousness seemed to evaporate from Justin's features, and Emily was relieved. They had barely made it into the house when he asked her if she was ready to hear the story. A hint of excitement could be heard in his voice as he addressed her.

"It sounds like you really believe that this story is important."

"Like I said, the tree is more than a monument or symbol. It is an actual living tree, or at least what was left of one after it was almost destroyed. Jaali, the jinni that did it, failed to kill the deep roots."

"Another myth?"

"No." He shook his head. "The tree is a very real part of our history and how we came to be here in the human realm."

"Is that why you didn't want to talk about this back there?"

"I wasn't sure how well the amulets would work or how long they would last. I didn't want to chance it."

He leaned forward in his seat and clasped his hands in front of him. "You already know that travel between the realms is supposed to be impossible, and you have seen that it takes an immense amount of power for most to accomplish."

She nodded. "That's why Amanda can only do it with both the boost from the runes on her back and the aid of her staff."

"Correct. Now, to understand the story, first you need to know that travel between the Emerald Mountains and the human realm has always been easier for the jinn.

"Although some jinni believe that the ease of travel is more closely related to our biology, legend says that it is because the jinn had a fondness for humans and that the goddesses allowed us to under certain circumstances.

"As such, in order to keep the peace and whatnot, those that wanted to go to the human realm would have to do an immense amount of studying and training. They would also have to promise they wouldn't interfere with humans before the jinn council would condone it."

"What do you believe, science or legend?"

"Maybe it's both." He shrugged. "What I believe isn't important. What is important, for your understanding, is that it would be considered an honor to be allowed to travel here, and adolescent jinn were willing to work very hard to do so."

Emily nodded to show that she understood.

"I will try to keep it short. Before the townspeople evacuated the Emerald Mountains, an arcane sorcerer somehow made it into the realm and kidnapped one of the younglings there, which set off a domino effect of panic amongst the inhabitants. Many of the jinn believed that if one of the arcane could make it into the Emerald Mountains, more would follow.

"It was decided that they would go against their traditions and beliefs to protect their youngsters. They would send them to the human realm.

"The problem was not all the youngsters had manifested the ability to travel in such a way or the desire to leave.

"Some of the elders knew of a tree that was fabled to have roots so deep, they connected the Emerald Mountains to the human realm, and they used it as a conduit to force the youths through.

"Among this group of younglings was a jinni named Jaali. He had witnessed the kidnapping first-hand, and he had wanted to be able to stay behind in order to fight back if more of the arcane showed up."

Emily offered a meek smile as Justin transferred his gaze from the floor to focus on her. "You see, besides being ripped from his home, he had lost two friends that day: the youngling that was kidnapped and the guardian that had been in charge of them.

Emily's smile faltered. "You don't think..."

"I do." Justin shifted in his seat. "I mean, it is the only story like that I have ever heard, apart from the one Amanda tells."

"Is it important to what's happening now?"

"I'm not sure. I believe that Amanda may have stumbled upon the very same jinni that was imprisoned in the story. Whether someone purposely placed the prison there for her to find or not remains a mystery."

"Well, tell me more about this young jinni."

"Jaali tried to bury his wrath inside, vowing to seek retribution. As time went by and he began to grow into adolescence, it started becoming apparent in his manifestations."

Emily cleared her throat before interrupting. "I have to admit, I am not positive what you mean by that."

"Jinni with ill intent often take on certain characteristics. In fact, the jinn even have a specific name for them. They refer to them as an ifrit."

"And you just grow into one?"

The excitement drained from his face. "Full blooded-jinni do not have a solid form at birth. It's hard for me to describe, because being half human, I never went through that type of change."

The more Emily got to know Justin, the more she realized that his half-blooded heritage seemed to bother him. "It's okay. I think I get it."

"Alright. I will continue then." He sat back in his seat. "The jinn from the town tried to help Jaali quell his anger by sending him back to the Emerald Mountains with one of the elders.

"One morning, the townspeople woke to the smell of smoke. It wasn't hard to determine the source. They had built their town around the tree, and it was burning. The elder that had accompanied Jaali lay unconscious in the grass nearby.

"They raced to put the fire out, but the tree had been engulfed in flames. They would have thought it was dead if they couldn't still feel magic emanating from it. They dug down into the ground until they found the point at the roots where the fire had not damaged them. Then, with the aid of a spell, they covered the tree in a layer of stone to help preserve it as best they could.

"Later, when the elder came to, he told the townspeople that they had found their village in the Emerald Mountains almost abandoned. Only a few jinn had not moved on. This affected Jaali in a way he hadn't predicted. Jaali became obsessed with the idea that the kidnapping had been his fault."

Emily scowled. "How would that be possible?"

"It's not, but sometimes you can't argue with grief, especially not when it's festered for so long."

His words reminded her of the people she had hurt in the past. Whether she had meant to harm them or not, it made no difference. Memories of them were always there in the back of her mind. "In his eyes, he was at least to a small extent responsible."

"Yes. You see, the guardian that had been tasked with watching the younglings was not being very attentive. His mind was on the fact that at that very moment the council was deciding if he had earned the privilege of going to human realm.

"Now, Jaali was not happy that he wanted to leave. He was very fond of this guardian, and he was worried that if he went to the human realm, he would never see him again. When it became apparent that his mind was elsewhere, Jaali saw his chance to keep him there. He knew that if anything happened to his charges, the council's decision would have to lean toward denying his trip."

"So he encouraged the other children, I mean younglings, to misbehave?"

"More or less, but the fact remained that although he noticed that the stranger's magic wasn't familiar to him, he was too young to know why. Nevertheless, Jaali said that he led the flock of younglings toward the stranger.

"Perhaps he thought that by his claim, the guardian that had been punished would be released. But magical imprisonment isn't that simple. The guardian had failed to protect the youngling, and that was that.

"Deciding that Jaali's ideas were bad for everyone there, the elder and the remaining jinn from the Emerald Mountains tried to force him to return the human realm with the aid of the ancient tree, and that's when he and the tree burst into flames."

"So, you don't really know if he burned it on purpose."

"I guess not. But that's not really the point of the story."

"Okay, okay."

# 29

# Amanda - The Climb

Amanda had wasted no time invoking her shadow magic as she exited the house. She had even felt a slight comfort from it as it swirled around her, removing her from the jinn village and from Kiami's grasp. It had been more of a challenge than she had expected, stopping the magic from funneling through the gemstone on her staff. She was so used to using it to control her power that it had become almost automatic.

When the shadowy tendrils released her, the mountain range still lay in the distance. The peak she sought rose up slightly higher than the others, but was much flatter at the top.

She dropped her staff at her feet and held her hands up to frame the view. It fit neatly in the square her fingers created, like a perfect photograph. She lifted her eyes skyward and blew a kiss toward the rising sun.

As the wind swirled around her, tousling her hair, she breathed in deeply and lectured herself. This wasn't a game. The mountains were far steeper than any she had seen in person before. They formed a great line against the horizon. The range was high to the west and low to the east, curling at the end like a tail.

She shifted the satchel that hung from her shoulders and reached down to retrieve her staff, wondering how far she could make it before nightfall. She tried not to think of the total distance between her and the top. She would just take one step at a time until they were all done.

The wind whispered a sweet melody as she trudged forward, and as the hours passed, she marveled in the solitude that surrounded her; it was so serene. The trees stood ghost-like, the lone observers of her trek.

The mountain itself was the only thing that called to her, and she realized how tired she had grown. This thing, she didn't even know what it was yet, held power over her, and she was bound by rules and regulations of this world she knew so little about.

When she reached the distance where the land began to swell up noticeably, a rocky trail appeared. The path seemed to snake up around the side of a mountain, with a sheer drop to the right. She kneeled in the grass by the trail's edge; she hadn't sought solitude on her journey to the mountain, but she had found it. Now she wished time would stop, allowing her to forget about everything else.

She rolled her eyes at her own thoughts. Someone would come for her eventually. The only way for her to get back to this state would be to continue her journey through to the end. She needed to see it finished.

The light was fading, the sun had begun to dip in the sky, and she yawned. Tendrils of iridescent silver mist seemed to creep over the mountainside. She thought of using magic to advance her journey, but remembered that the higher she climbed, the colder it would be, and this spot reminded her of a place she had once camped out with her father before everything had changed.

To her surprise, the thought of her father didn't sting quite as much as it had in the past, so instead of pushing the memory away, she smiled and tried to enjoy it.

She pulled on the coat she had borrowed in preparation for the night, and with renewed determination, she began to walk in a wide circle around the trail's opening, looking for fallen twigs and branches to start a fire.

She was going to stay here for the night, watching as the sky turned dark and became speckled with silver stars. In the morning, she would concentrate on her journey, but for now she would forget about the world she had been thrust into for just a little bit longer.

It had been hard for her to get going again in the morning, even with the thoughts of avenging her losses and finding the creature that had started this whole thing, because in truth, she didn't know what she would find at the top. She knew it could just as easily be disappointment as anything else. So, as she climbed, she made a game of coming up with different motivations for reaching the highest point beyond her lust for redemption and revenge.

For one, she knew at the very least that she wanted to see the panorama from the mountain's crown, and when she tired of envisioning that, she tried to think of the mountain as a giant beast that had lain down one day in an enchanted sleep and never gotten up.

Perhaps its bones still made up the interior of the mountain, and its essence still resided deep at its center. Perchance that was really what Bloise had sent her to find all along.

She giggled as she plodded upward. *Why not?* she thought. She could believe that just as easily as anything else she had learned since she had discovered the truth of the world.

Then she bit at her tongue. She could also believe much worse things were waiting for her at the highest heights and inside the heart of the mountain.

By the afternoon, she heard the familiar babble of water gurgling in the distance, and it was music to her ears. Her feet had begun to feel sore from the relentless climb, and she longed to feel the cold water move over her skin like a healing salve, removing the irritation, even if only for a few minutes. But from the information she had found, it looked as though the river moved along the mountain, away from the trail, and she knew leaving the trail would not be a smart move. She pushed the idea of going to the river from her mind.

She decided that she had made the right choice soon after. A short distance later, as she moved on down the trail, she began to see the first signs of frost in the air and on the ground. She pulled on her pilfered gloves and hat from the bag.

Before long, the dark green of the pines was coated in a crystalline snow, and with every step, she heard the soft crunch it made underfoot.

She could have stood there drinking it all in, listening to the silence that hung so thickly all around her, but throughout the day, the air had begun to grow more frigid and become thinner the higher she climbed. It was time to make tracks if she wanted to reach the crown before nightfall.

As the level of the white pristine powder inched up past her ankles, the wind began to whip harshly around Amanda, screaming through the chilly air. She scolded herself for being in such a hurry to leave. She wished she was more appropriately dressed for the climb, spiked shoes and a pickaxe, maybe a woolen scarf. Something to help with her footing and to keep the chill from creeping in under her coat.

Her face felt cold and wind-burned. She was sure that if she could look in a mirror at that moment, it would appear a bright red. She touched her gloved hands to her cheeks, but the frozen material did little to help.

"Not too much farther now," she hummed to herself. She hadn't realized how little she knew about scaling a mountain of this magnitude. Her past hiking adventures had not prepared her as much as she had thought.

This time, she didn't give leaving the trail a second thought as she spotted a group of trees not too far off in the distance and bolted toward it, seeking a few moments escape from the wind.

The low pines formed a tight circle, effectively blocking the brunt of its force, and she collapsed to her knees. She pulled off her gloves and placed the warmer flesh onto her cheeks, trying to feel whatever warmth they could offer.

After several minutes without much of a change, she stuffed her hands back into the coverings. She tried to force the edges of her hat down farther onto her face and wondered at the possibility of starting a small fire. Maybe, she thought, she could last the night inside her small barrier without freezing to death or catching the trees ablaze.

"Fat chance," she mumbled.

A new noise invaded the drone of wind that she had become used to, causing her to hop back to her feet and peer around the side of the tree closest to her. Something had changed. The wind had slowed, and a peculiar rustling could be heard from somewhere close by. She was sure it wasn't the echo of the river in the distance. It sounded closer to the crunch her own feet had made as she moved along the trail, only not quite the same. After what she assumed would be the noise from the initial step, it was more like a tearing sound, as if something was being dragged through the crisp snow.

Pain ripped through her with such a sudden force that she doubled over, clutching at her abdomen as a loud scream tore from her. She had been so focused on the strange noise that she hadn't noticed the world around her waver as she was forced behind someone else's eyes.

She knew it was Kiami, she could tell by the wild hair blowing around her face and the bare feet that dug into the snow.

*Foot*, she corrected herself. There was only one visible foot. The thoughts that radiated inside her mind were jumbled with torment as she stared down at the untransformed limb, still twisted into the shape of a talon and yet covered in her human skin.

Pain radiated from every inch of her host's body, and it was all Amanda could do to try to push past it.

Kiami was stuck in agony, and for the moment, Amanda was stuck with her. She had no way of escaping the vision. She would have to let it play out and then hope that she still had the energy to find out what had happened.

She could see that Kiami was on the trail she had taken. Some of her own footprints were still visible along the path. She knew there had been a chance Kiami would try to follow to the mountain. But she felt angrier at her for it at that moment than she would have thought possible.

Kiami made a sudden move away from the trail and fumbled forward as her unchanged appendage made contact with something hard. Amanda caught a familiar glimpse of the trees she had taken shelter behind rush past as her host's body crumpled forward into a pile on the snow, her cloak twisting around her as she landed.

She noticed that the cold barely affected Kiami, and if not for the excruciating pain radiating from her, Amanda would have cherished the few moments reprieve from the frosty air.

It took her host several minutes before she sat up and uncovered the thing that had tripped her. To Amanda's shock, it was her very own staff. It had been partly covered in the snow, and in Kiami's pain-ridden state, she had not noticed it until it was too late.

She realized she must have dropped it in her hurry to seek the cover of the trees, while her own body was in distress. She didn't have time to scold herself as a fresh bolt of pain shot through her host. Kiami had lifted the staff, and as she used it to push herself up off the ground, Amanda's vision became blurry. All went black for a few seconds, and then she was thrust back behind her own eyes.

# 30

## Kiami - Long Trip Down

Anger and admiration coursed through Kiami's veins, confusing her pain-addled mind. If Amanda hadn't been in such a rush, she wouldn't have hurried after her, and none of this would have happened.

She couldn't remember a time when she had felt such discomfort and distress.

Kiami had decided long ago that she looked up to Amanda, who had been forced into a dark apprenticeship, at least in a sense, and lied to. She had been humiliated, pushed to do bad things, made to make unfathomable decisions, and she wanted justification... Redemption.

Kiami gulped. She felt that Amanda had to make some very hard choices, and she had never thought to blame her for letting it change her inside. In fact, deep down, she had questioned if she could have endured in the same way.

Now, in her current state, she found herself wondering if Amanda had really changed as much on the inside as she believed she had, or if she was just being the person she thought she needed to be to make it through. Unlike Amanda, most of the things she did were deeply ingrained within her.

She was a hunter, but it was an instinct. A necessity for survival that she learned from her owl persona. The more she felt her own guilt, pain, and suffering, the less she could call up reasons to condone Amanda's rash actions in her own mind.

Kiami leaned on the staff, clutching her fingers around in a tight grip. Right now, she wanted to take that staff into the trees where she knew Amanda waited, and she wanted to bring it down as hard as she could on her head.

But she wouldn't. It didn't matter how angry she became. It just wasn't who she was. Even in her current state, she was still able to make reasonable decisions.

It was Amanda's fault that she was here, but it hadn't been her that caused Kiami to be in the predicament she now found herself in.

She had done it to herself, and she knew it.

She could sense something was off before she attempted to change back, but she had ignored it and pushed anyway, refusing to give up, even when nothing happened. She tried again, forcing it to start, but only the pain was instant as she felt bones contort in a sluggish and uncomfortable way. It was as if the magic was working in slow motion for a full minute, then it just petered out altogether, and she was left in some kind of strange hybrid limbo.

Kiami had never flown so long and so far without changing back into human form. She hadn't even taken time to recharge at all. She shouldn't have pushed herself so much.

Now she barely remembered why she had thought her news would make a difference. Amanda was on a mission, and she wasn't going to let anything stop her. She hadn't even bothered to take the time to tell Emily that she was leaving.

She dropped the staff just outside of the group of trees. Why wasn't Amanda coming out from her hiding spot? *Maybe she is trying to ignore me.*

Kiami balled her hands into fists and opened her mouth to sing; Amanda was going to come out and hear what she had to say, whether she wanted to or not.

Within seconds, Amanda appeared from behind the trees. The sight of her almost caused Kiami to lose her concentration. Her face looked chapped and crimson, and her movements were much stiffer than they should have been as she attempted to follow the music, imitating the dance. As Kiami sang, she felt her energy returning, little by little.

Kiami bent down and picked up the staff, realizing it was a good reason for Amanda to stay and listen. Kiami tied the staff against her back using the long cords that had protruded from the cloak's hood. Then she moved farther away from her, with purpose. She wanted the song to last a little bit longer. She swayed up the trail, her own movements becoming easier as her body completed her transition into human form.

She knew that Amanda's main thoughts would be to follow, at least until she stopped her song. As far as she knew, the idea would repeat in her head as she trailed after her up the mountainside, almost oblivious of her own anger at the situation. Then Kiami could show her that there was nothing at the top, and there could be no argument. She hoped that Amanda would be in a forgiving mood at the end of the trip.

When she had flown above the uppermost rocks at dawn, she saw no sign of anything but snow. When she had seen that nothing awaited Amanda, she thought that it would be a good day. Now she knew better.

Flying above the mountain and climbing up were two very different experiences. She almost forgot to continue her song as she reached forward, still trying to maintain the rhythm of the music as she pulled herself upward.

While out loud she was singing to Amanda, a different mantra reverberated in her head. Just one-foot hold, one handhold at a time, no more, no less. It was a difficult balance to maintain. She wrapped her fingers around the next rocky outcrop, making firm contact. Her mind only had room for victory and the next movement of each limb.

She wasn't sure how much time had passed before Amanda charged at her. The song had ceased to emanate from her throat. To do to the juggling act she had been trying to perform, she assumed.

She had never attempted something like it before and was happy that it had lasted as long as it did. She may have been able to manage balancing the deep concentration needed to scale the mountain while keeping Amanda under her spell if she had not left her moonstone at Emily's, but she had removed it from her neck after they returned from Bloise's as a precaution. She knew no matter how much time passed, she would never be able to forget what had happened to the boy on the beach.

She hadn't even noticed when Amanda had stopped pulling herself up along the rocks behind her, but she could see her, tapping her warn boot on the ledge above her, as Kiami moved to pull herself up just before she struck.

There was only a few feet of ledge, and it was icy and snow-covered. Kiami stared down over the edge. From here, the river water appeared to be green-tinged and entirely without motion. Despite the relentless sun rays, it would be cold and deep. She shuddered, happy that she hadn't toppled over the side when Amanda barreled into her, but troubled by her thoughts.

These slopes that gave a home to so much life, a foundation for trees and shrubs, grass, and ferns, could take it as well, and had she been in the same weakened state as Amanda, she could have learned about it first-hand. Her song had not only helped her finish her transformation, but had also renewed her energy.

Now Amanda sat cross-legged on the ledge, with her face buried in her hands.

She whispered only one word to Kiami as she lifted her face. "Why?"

"Why what?"

"Take your pick." Anger seeped out, and her voice rose an octave with each word. "Why would you come here? Why would you cause yourself such harm, and why would you do that to me?"

Kiami took a step back as Amanda rose, her fists clenched at her sides. She no longer looked beaten and battered. Her eyes were wild with anger, and the fury seemed to invigorate her.

"I'm sorry, I—I didn't know what else to do."

"You didn't know what else to do?" Amanda laughed eerily. "Stay put, that's what you were supposed to do, not half kill yourself trying to get here."

Even when Amanda had dragged her through the woods, she hadn't been afraid for her safety, but now, the hair prickled on the back of her neck.

"I don't care about the blank pages. There is something here that I need to see, and you can't be here."

Kiami straightened up. "You can't just push people out of the way to keep them safe. That's not how it works."

"So, what's your plan? You hunt me down and force me to go back by controlling me with your song?"

"I only wanted to show you that there was nothing up here."

"I didn't expect there to be a big gold door with flashing lights, Kiami."

"This is a bad place, Amanda. My mom..." Kiami gulped back the rest of her words as Amanda stepped closer.

Her face twisted. She wasn't just angry; she was hurt. "Your mom? Which one? As far as I can tell, neither of those women you called your guardians were really your mom, were they? So how do you know that they wanted what was best for you?"

With Amanda's face only inches away from her own, Kiami's breath caught in her throat, and she tried to step backward. Instead, her foot slid sideways down the ridge. Instinctively, she reached forward and grabbed on to Amanda's coat with one hand.

Her eyes went wide for a moment as Amanda tipped forward in surprise before regaining her footing.

Kiami felt her cape shuffle around her body in the breeze. The staff hit against her back and twisted loose from the fabric and cords, sliding down past her legs into the unknown.

"Stop struggling or you will lose your grip," Amanda yelled as she wrapped her fingers around her outstretched arm. "Can you change form?"

Kiami closed her eyes tight, willing her legs to stay as still and as straight as possible as she reached for a rock with her free hand. She felt for her magic, but nothing happened. "I don't think so."

Her fingers slid against the wet stone, and she inched them back up, trying to tighten them around it again. As the rock came loose, she felt Amanda's hand wrap tight against her wrist, encompassing it with the fingers of her outstretched arm, just as the soft noise of tearing fabric met her sensitive ears.

Amanda lurched forward another step, but gave a quick pull on Kiami's arm back toward the center of the cliff, giving her just enough room to get both her feet planted onto the ridge before losing her footing again.

This time Amanda stumbled forward on the ice, both of her feet sliding past the outcropping, forcing her into a sitting position and over the side.

Kiami threw herself onto her stomach, grasping at Amanda's exposed arm. She felt her nails tear into her flesh. The borrowed coat lay in tatters somewhere behind them.

She tried to stretch the fingertips on her other hand down to Amanda, but she couldn't quite make it.

She could feel warm blood trickling against her hand, and she looked over the edge at the puncture marks that her nails caused.

Amanda looked away from her as she tried to meet her eyes and shouted, "Let go, Kiami."

Instead, she dug her nails in deeper and pushed herself to change. She didn't need to transform all the way; she just needed wings to pull them away from the dangerous rocks and slow their fall.

At first, the magic only fizzled, and then a scream tore from her as she started to transform in slow motion again, this time from human to owl form.

She yelled out in pain as she felt pressure pushing and pulling at her shoulder blades. The flesh on her back tore as her bones contorted. She inched closer to the edge with her free arm and pushed herself over, grabbing toward Amanda with every muscle she could feel as they both plunged downward.

# 31

# Amanda - Riverside

Amanda could feel the crisp air whip around them as they broke free from the ledge. Kiami had used her weight to push them out just far enough beyond the jutting sides, or they would have crashed into them in an instant. For a moment she felt the warmth of Kiami's embrace against her exposed skin, and she returned the embrace as she watched them descend together back toward the side of the mountain.

Then another swoosh of cold air engulfed her as they changed direction. The beat of Kiami's wings made a loud whoosh noise in Amanda's ears as they began to lift up higher from the mountain. She could hear Kiami's heart thudding, the rhythm irregular and strained.

Amanda squeezed her eyes shut. She knew that Kiami hadn't had the energy to change all the way, and the memory of her earlier experience with that was still fresh in her mind.

It wasn't worth the torture she was putting herself through. Amanda let go, and she could feel Kiami's trembling muscles as she tried to hang on to her.

A screech rang out from Kiami, more owl than human, as she felt herself slide from her arm, and Amanda waited to be engulfed by rushing air as she fell. Instead, she felt pressure at her waist as Kiami clenched her around the hips.

She let out a howl as the nails dug through her light clothing, penetrating her flesh and rubbing against her bone.

"Let go." The words came out like a low growl, but she knew Kiami could hear her. She flexed her talons, and Amanda bit her lip against the stinging pain to hold in a whimper. She meant business. This was just as painful for her; in fact, worse.

Kiami let out another pained screech, and they shifted downward as if she had lost control.

*She's going to kill herself,* Amanda thought. "What if you get stuck like this?" she shrieked.

A sudden jerk upward stopped their descent again. She could feel her boots skim the top of the water, and she sucked in her breath before looking up at Kiami's half-changed form. The pain was evident on her features. It was a spectacle, this creature with the wings of an owl and two large talons for feet.

Amanda contemplated which part of her was really in charge. She was scary-looking and lovely at the same instant. Her silvery eyes shone, like turbulent waves against the seashore's edge on a gray-skyed day. She cocked her head at an odd angle, one that no human could have accomplished; Amanda had seen owls do it, but it was disconcerting to see Kiami do it now.

They seemed to be following the flow of the river. "Drop me now. I have to do this part alone."

Kiami opened her mouth, but only a raspy wheezing sound escaped.

Amanda took in a deliberate, deep breath to help slow down her own thudding heart. "I have one last secret to share, Kiami, and you are not going to like it."

Kiami cocked her head to the other side and looked down at her, and Amanda wondered if she could still understand her words, or if the pain was too much. "Jacqueline didn't leave you."

"Liar," she wheezed back and began to cough.

Amanda squeezed her eyes shut and bellowed, "Why can't you just hate me? Don't you get it! I banished her to the jinn realm! She didn't leave you!"

For a moment there was nothing, and then Amanda opened her eyes, and everything seemed to move in slow motion. Water again skimmed the top of her dangling boots as Kiami's clutch loosened and then released her into the icy river.

Amanda didn't look back up to see what direction Kiami took; she hadn't had time before the frigid water enveloped her entire body. She screamed as the water washed over her head, and she got a mouthful of the foul-tasting liquid.

She felt something solid beneath her heavy boots and pushed herself back up above the surface. She spun her head around, knowing that the shore couldn't be that far, but her vision seemed blurred, and when she tried to straighten her legs back out, she couldn't find the bottom with her feet.

She began to tread water, and her head managed to stay above the surface of the caressing river. She attempted to push herself forward toward the shore, but it was as if the river didn't want to let her go, just as Kiami hadn't wanted to.

Each advancing movement was countered, and she felt as if she was being pulled back toward the center, groped at by some unseen force as the river itself attempted to stuff her head back under.

Terror hit her then, and her throat constricted. She held her breath and allowed herself to sink back below the surface. This anguish was too much to bear. She needed oxygen. The water no longer felt cold to her, and she knew she was in shock.

Her lungs began to burn, and she let out the air in slow, controlled bursts. She tried to move back up above the surface, but it seemed an impossible task.

She wanted to give in to the desire to breathe; the intensity of the craving to do so was increasing. She knew she could simply let the water accumulate in her lungs. Eventually, the craving would literally be irresistible anyway, and she would have no choice but to breathe in the water, allowing it to pass into her airways.

She wasn't sure how long she fought against the river before her head popped back up above the surface. She sucked in greedy gulps of air as she kicked her legs beneath her.

She continued to tread water, even as the world around her faded and then snapped back into focus. The realization that she was losing consciousness intermittently caused her to slow her efforts and allow the panic to pass. Her body was giving up the fight against the water. It wasn't surrender or acceptance; it simply was.

At least she wouldn't have to watch the others die, she thought, and for a moment she was relieved. The weight would be lifted from her.

Something solid collided with her body and groped at her shoulders, but she could no longer kick her legs or open her eyes.

Amanda shivered uncontrollably as she rolled to her side, spewing water. When she was able to take a full breath, she tried to lean into a sitting position, but her exhaustion was so complete that her soaked clothing weighed her down. Her vision still seemed obscured, and she couldn't see who had dragged her to the shore.

"Do you remember what happened?" She didn't recognize the voice that spoke to her, but there was something familiar about the person.

She clutched at her burning throat as she tried to speak, but no sound escaped. She attempted to sit up again, causing another painful coughing fit as her lungs tried to expel any liquid remnants that still lingered. Just as the coughing slowed, her abdomen exploded with hot, searing pain, and she leaned forward as she vomited.

When she was finished, her rescuer grabbed her by the arms and pulled her a few feet away from the mess. "It took all of me to save you. I didn't have anything left to send to Kiami. I need to check on her."

Amanda could feel the coarse ground scrape against her cheek as she gave a weak nod. Still lying flat in the dirt, she tried to move her hand closer to her face. Her fingers tingled with the effort.

Instead of her eyes focusing on her fingertips as she drew them near to her face, she saw a fuzzy flash of blue light, and then the world around her fell into darkness, only this time instead of death, it felt like sleep.

When she opened her eyes again, her vision seemed to have returned to normal. In front of her, a circular pile of cinder and ash was surrounded by a small wall of stone. The fire had been positioned just outside the small entrance to a cave. With effort, she pulled her sore body up into a sitting position and poked at the edge of the remains. It had gone cold some time ago.

Her clothes were dry, but she felt chilled through to the bone. Behind her she found a thick gray piece of fabric. The material seemed to be roughly twice the size of her, and she assumed that it had been draped over her like a blanket at some point. She pulled it toward her and wrapped it around herself.

Amanda was glad that enough dim light made its way into the cave for her to see her surroundings. She looked up at the cave ceiling; it wasn't very high. If she had the energy to stand, she doubted she would even be able to without hitting her head on the hard stone. The cave was much wider than it was tall. With the entrance being its skinniest point, it got wider the farther back she looked and then rounded off in a pear shape.

Her heart leapt into her throat when she saw her staff and satchel lying against the cave walls. She leaned over as far as she could and yanked the bag toward herself. She couldn't help but grimace as she pulled out a water bottle to take a few sips. She knew she needed it, but the idea of purposely swallowing it made her stomach flop. As she tilted the container over her mouth, the liquid stung the outside of her dry, cracked lips.

Amanda knew that if she ever hoped to regain her energy, she needed to eat something. She reached back into the satchel and found a granola bar. She pulled tiny pieces off it and ate them bit by teeny bit. She didn't want the food to come back up.

Next, she pulled the flashlight out and clutched it to her chest as she lay back down on the cave floor. She couldn't tell if the sun was rising or setting, and she didn't want to wake back up to find herself without a source of light at hand.

# 32

# Kiami - Whispers

As dusk settled around her, the wind howled through the landscape, causing icicles to clink together like wind chimes. Kiami shivered. Even though she barely felt the cold, it was a haunting but beautiful place. It felt almost otherworldly. The sun blazed overhead, despite the fact that she could see her breath each time she exhaled the crisp air.

The pain from her last half transformation still lingered below the surface of her flesh, yet she couldn't bring herself to get up and sing. She had caused this affliction to herself in order to save Amanda, and now she didn't even know if she was alive or if she had drowned in the river. She had planned on returning to the water to locate Amanda right away, but she had begun to doubt herself.

Kiami wondered if there was something wrong with her. She hadn't wanted to let Amanda go. Not even after she made her announcement. Doing so had not been her first instinct, but she knew it was what Amanda wanted her to do.

She hadn't gone far from the river. She only flew long enough so that she knew Amanda wouldn't be able to see her as she landed. She pulled her knees up to her chest and held them, her cloak settled around her haphazardly.

# ENDOW

She hadn't been sleeping when the wisps came. But she did have her eyes closed tight as she envisioned Amanda falling into the river over and over.

The familiar blue balls of smoke had gotten her attention by tugging at her hair, and when she opened her eyes to see what was causing the irritation, she couldn't even bring herself to offer a smile.

She hadn't experienced nearly as many interactions with the wisp creatures as Amanda and Emily, and she wondered how they were able to grasp things, given their semitransparent appearance.

She released the hold she had on her knees and waved at the apparitions. She needed guidance, and from what the others had said, these things had been quite helpful to them in the past. As she watched several of them zig-zag in front of her, she realized that there were more coming toward her by the second.

They appeared both from behind the trees and above them, collecting a short distance ahead of her as if she was a beacon. She tried to count them, but they were moving so fast that she couldn't be sure if she was adding the same wisp multiple times.

She could only estimate that at the point when more stopped appearing, there were thirty or so within her line of sight. She lowered her knees and sat up straighter as the fist-sized balls started colliding with one another and merging together. Before long, they formed one mass hovering a few feet in front of her.

No one had ever mentioned this happening when they had shared their encounters, but she stayed still, trying to be patient.

The mass inched closer to her, and as it did the shape began to change, morphing into a human-like form. Kiami's eyes grew wide as she watched its transparency diminish. She could still almost see through the figure, but it had lost the smoky swirling effect and darkened in color significantly, leading her to believe that it had solidified, at least partially. Although the face of the being appeared blurred, she could make out the bump of a nose, the outline of a mouth, and indented sockets where eyes should be.

She covered her mouth with her hand in astonishment and then removed it again to speak as realization settled in. "You're one of us, aren't you?" What other explanation could there be?

The being nodded as it sat down in front of her. "You can call me Blaine."

Kiami had not expected to hear words come from the mouth shape, and she raised her eyebrows in surprise.

"Forgive my appearance." Blaine lifted a hand and indicated the area where his face had not formed fully. "I had to send part of myself somewhere else."

Kiami looked down at her taloned feet and moved the muscles in her back that helped her wings to flex. She looked like a monster herself. She lifted her mouth into a smile. "I can forgive yours if you can be okay with mine."

The corners of the strange mouth outline lifted into a half circle. "Deal."

"So, you are the wisps?"

"Well, I am half human, as we all are. I, unlike the others, never really managed to achieve the full appearance of one."

"I'm sorry."

"Don't be. It is so much easier for me to move around as the wisps of energy, and I can, in essence, be in more than one place at a time. I mean, sending off a few parts of me here and there does have disadvantages, but I think the advantages by far outweigh them."

"I gather that you have never shown this form to Amanda or Emily, so why are you showing yourself to me now? I am curious."

"Well, I did just come from Amanda, in my full form. Although she was in no state to recognize me."

Kiami gulped. "Was she okay?"

"She will be." Blaine's form shrugged. "To answer your original question, it has never been necessary in the past. Right now, I think it's better if I keep my interactions to a minimum, but it seemed to be the only way that I could try to help you. When I found you here today, you appeared to be fighting with yourself about something you can't control."

"What do you mean?"

"Try as you might, Kiami, you can't control the way you feel about someone. Mask it, maybe, sure."

"How do you know what I was thinking about?"

"I can't read your mind, if that's what you're implying. I see a lot, though. Sometimes more than I want to." Blaine gave a light chuckle.

She looked down at the ground. "I know I should hate her. Is there something wrong with me?"

"Well now," he placed his hand on his chin, "she believes what she did to Jacqueline is unforgivable. Why don't you?"

She mulled it over. Given the circumstances, it seemed to her that Amanda had probably saved Jacqueline's life by banishing her. "She didn't kill her. She may have even saved her life by sending her away."

"See now? That makes sense to me. So why are you struggling with it?"

"If I tell the others, they will think I am crazy."

"It's always best not to make assumptions, Kiami. I think the more they see, the more they understand her. You cannot expect good all the time, when everything around you has gone bad."

"Do you think Amanda will ever find peace?"

"I can't answer that."

"It's like every time she loses someone or something, she leaves a piece of herself behind."

"Sometimes it's necessary to get lost in the dark before you can truly find yourself."

"What if there is no coming back for her?"

"Will it change the way you feel?"

"I would run through fire for her. It scares me."

"Love is not a thing that you can choose. For instance, Jacqueline and your mom, they fell in love with you the moment they saw you. There was no question in their minds that they needed to protect you and teach you."

"You knew them?"

"Not in an official capacity. You could call me an eavesdropper, I guess, if that can make sense for you."

His suggestion that he had been watching since she was first placed with her guardians threw her off a bit, and she couldn't help but wonder how long he had been interfering below the radar.

She knew better than to think it wasn't possible for him to have been around long before that. She had first-hand knowledge that they didn't all age at the same rate. She had grown much more rapidly than a human would have, and jinn, she had learned, aged much slower.

"Now is not the right time for further explanations."

"You're leaving?"

He moved his head up and down. "I have to attend to something else. Don't worry, I know you don't like secrets. If it feels right, you can tell them about me. I will see you again soon, all of you. But I do need you to do something for me."

"What's that?"

"Promise me you will let her do what she needs to do. Promise me you will stay away."

"But she could be in danger."

"This is something she has to do alone. She will be back when the time is right. You have to help Emily and Justin now."

"What if we can't find the others? What if we can't manage without her?"

"I believe, and that's enough to push me to go on. You need to believe."

"I did. I do. It just keeps getting harder. What if we aren't enough?" She knew his words were meant to make her feel better, but she wasn't sure anything would unfog her mind right now.

"Think about it, Kiami. The puppeteer is afraid of us. Why? Because we are enough, and he knows it."

After Blaine left, she picked herself up off the snowy ground and shook out her cape. She wanted to trust in everything he said, but her optimism was still waning. She reminded herself of what she had told Amanda about taking one thing at a time.

Before she could do anything else, she needed to get her energy back and finish her transformation.

She walked toward the river, secretly hoping to catch a glimpse of Amanda as she followed it. She was sure that Blaine would be none the wiser. The possibility of her still being around the river was slim anyway, she assured herself, and if she did happen to see Amanda, she wouldn't attempt an approach.

She didn't start to sing until she could hear the roar of the rushing, ever-flowing water. She approached the riverbank and continued into the liquid, staring down at the stones that were settled at the bottom. They were many shades of brown, gray, and white. Some even appeared to have a reddish tint.

The water at the point she stood had a current that tugged at her calves, begging her to step in deeper. She didn't really expect to see Amanda near the river, but she knew the river was created by the melting snow at the mountain's peak where she assumed Amanda had been heading.

She had thought maybe she would see a sign or get a sense of her from it, something for her to cling to, but her hunting instincts failed her. There was no indication, visible or otherwise, of what route Amanda had chosen to travel.

She inched further in, slowly soaking the hem of her clothes and willing herself to finish the transformation, only instead of being an owl, she pushed at her magic to turn her back to her full human form.

She had made a decision. She was going to take her time coming down the mountain, making sure she had fully restored her strength before she attempted to return to Emily, as Blaine had asked, and hoping she would see a sign from Amanda.

When the change was complete, she made her way up to the shore. Her damp clothing clung to her legs as she moved. It didn't matter which way she chose to descend, so she decided to walk with the sun at her back on the way down as she sung.

## 33

## Emily - Intuition

Time seemed to stand still for her since Kiami and Amanda had left. It felt as if she and Justin were stuck in a loop. The jinn hadn't returned, Etzion hadn't come back, and she had no idea when Kiami or Amanda would show up.

Each night, her dreams were a wrestling match. She couldn't help but feel that both the girls had put themselves in danger. As each day with no sign of them passed, she reminded herself that they weren't weak.

She thought maybe it was the smell of Justin's house that brought her unrest. After days of cleaning and scrubbing, the scent of fire was still prevalent, so each night they returned to Nina's to sleep. No matter what they cleaned with or how much stuff they threw away from the upstairs, it lingered. She refused to sleep there, and even though she knew Justin wanted to, he wouldn't leave her alone overnight.

Contributing her unease to that was easier than letting scenarios of the two of them in terrible situations run through her mind. She was also sure deep down it didn't help that once again she felt like she was biding her time until she had to leave.

Although, she reminded herself, this was not the same as before. She wasn't being forced out for being different. She had a mission. They had a task they were supposed to complete together.

Regardless of that, her old fears still returned, poking at her, and she had started bringing her red backpack with her each day before they left Nina's.

She wished she didn't feel like she needed to keep it close. She had thought that she would never use it again the last time she hung it on the back of the door to her room. It had been right after the people of town shared their secret with her.

Having it near her did have its advantages. On one trip, she had used it to smuggle the wooden book that she had taken from the Arcane realm back to her house without Justin seeing it. Then, during another one of their cleaning sprees, she had taken Etzion's gemstone from the drawer of the dresser before they had hefted the piece of furniture up and out of the house to be discarded. She hadn't considered Justin's guest room to be a safe hiding place to begin with, and she felt slightly better knowing it was with them.

She had placed it, still wrapped in the towel, in her red backpack, along with her and Justin's stones, since they were trying not to use them. While they were out, she didn't let the backpack leave her sight.

Thoughts tumbled around in her head as she tossed and turned. She hadn't gotten much sleep, and the room was already glowing with the faint orange light of the coming dawn.

She bit at her lip and sprang up. How would Etzion find them if he did return?

It was all she could think about as she readied herself for the day. She knew Justin wouldn't be back yet from his early morning trek deeper into town.

Each dawn before they ventured to his house, he would travel into the town center in order to make sure the magic he had used on the stone tree was holding and to look for signs that the jinn had returned. When he was satisfied, he would meet her back here so that they could start the cleaning regimen all over again.

Several blue wisps hovered in front of her when she opened the door to leave her room, and she couldn't help but grin at them. She hadn't seen any wisps since they had appeared in the Arcane realm, while they were searching for Kiami. Despite the fact that not much time had passed, it still felt like it had been too long since they appeared to her. They darted around her, and she turned to follow them back through.

Emily didn't have many possessions beyond the necessities of day-to-day life and the few items that she had carried in her red backpack when she had fled the beach. She had since picked up some outfits, books, and an old silver camera she had yet to use.

She couldn't recall what had drawn her to pick up the camera and look at it on the day she bought it. She had been wandering around in one of the small local shops.

It looked old to her, but when the clerk promised her it worked, she had taken his word. Before she left, he even went out of his way to show her how to load the film cartridge. Beyond that quick lesson, she didn't have much experience using one. Her parents hadn't ever shown any interest in taking pictures, even before her change.

That's where the four orbs hovered now, casting their blue light over the silver shell. Emily raised her eyebrows. "You want me to take a picture? How can that help anything?" She reached for the camera and inspected it.

She was certain it couldn't be of aid with the missing jinn, or Amanda and Kiami. She chewed at her lower lip and furrowed her brow. "For Etzion?" She wondered if a picture would work. She wasn't sure. Amanda had mentioned that he teleported to places he had been by calling up an image in his mind.

The orbs zigged and zagged in front of her, as if they were impatient. "I guess it's worth a try. If it helps Etzion find us more easily."

The wisps stayed close behind as she made her way to the front of the house and snapped a photo. When the instant film popped out, she held it in front of her, waiting for the image to form. She doubted the front of the house would be enough for him to find them if he couldn't teleport with the image, and leaving a note with a full explanation seemed dangerous.

Emily ran inside to investigate Nina's small desk and sifted through the drawers until she found a marker.

With a plan to tack the photo right to the wall in Justin's guest room, she wrote *TOWN* in thick black ink under the now fully developed photo.

As she turned to thank the wisps for the inspiration, she wasn't entirely surprised to find that they were nowhere to be seen.

# 34

# Amanda - Downward Spiral

Amanda couldn't remember how many times she had repeated the cycle, waking, drinking, eating, and then feeling the overwhelming desire to stay right where she was before allowing herself to drift back into a restful slumber.

Wrappers and water bottles littered the area around her, and she moved to scoop them all back into her satchel. She wondered how many days had passed, although it didn't seem that important right now.

She had never expected her rescuer to return. Something about the encounter had sat in the back of her mind. It was an unspoken understanding between them that when the figure had said they were going to check on Kiami, it was as if they had said, *"Your journey is not for me or her to make."*

She returned the flashlight and flung her satchel behind her shoulders. She crawled toward her staff on her hands and knees. At the moment, the ornament of power felt more like a burden than anything else. She sighed as she reached for it then dropped her hand.

Next to her staff, an arrow had been drawn on the floor with black charcoal or the end of a burnt stick. The arrow didn't look worn, but fresh. It couldn't have been there long, or it would have been wiped away, at least partially. She could only surmise that her rescuer had left it for her.

Amanda examined the back of the cave wall where the arrow pointed. A portion of the wall there was not solid, but individual rocks had been piled into place and pushed backward into a hole to block it.

She prodded at the rocks. They seemed to be wedged in pretty tight. She sat back on her heels, wondering if she was ready. She had a pretty good idea of where the hole would lead if she chose to uncover it. The only place it could: down into the mountain.

It was the place she had been intending to go all along. But now she hesitated, wondering if it was truly what she wanted. No. She shook her head. It was what she needed, to meet the puppeteer face to face.

She grabbed her staff and slipped the smaller end between the curved edges of two fist-sized rocks, trying to create enough leverage to pop one of them loose. The job took much less force than she had imagined, and as one rock loosened, tumbling forward, the rest fell out of place, sliding down around her knees.

The hole that had opened was only about three feet in diameter. Amanda did not like the idea of slinking down a tunnel that small. She stared at the opening for a moment, wondering why it seemed to be her fate to travel back down into another hole under the ground. She dreaded the idea; she had no way of knowing how far the tunnel went or if it really connected to the interior of the cave.

She turned it around in her mind, thinking of the way the roots of the ruined trees were said to connect the realms. She was going. She had to find out. If the cave tunnel didn't connect to the interior, then why would anyone have bothered drawing the arrow?

Her shoes felt oddly loose, and she moved to tighten them against her feet. They were a rough sight. The laces were frayed so much that they dangled in shreds at the sides, causing the tongue to hang down over the front of the shoes. They wouldn't remain on her feet for long if she crawled with them on through the tunnel.

She pulled them off and set them by the opening, thankful that even though it would be a clumsy and uncomfortable journey, the tunnel was wide enough that she wouldn't have to squeeze through it.

She grabbed her staff and laid it on the floor of the opening. She would have to drag it in along with her as she crawled on her hands and knees.

She had only moved a few yards when she came to another hole, similar in size and shape to the one she had gone through. Amanda ducked down, slid through, and then assessed her hands and feet for damage. She wasn't surprised to see them littered with small cuts and scratches.

The knuckles on the hand that held the staff had scraped painfully across the rough stone surface with each push forward, and a few times she had moved the tops of her bare feet over a small, jutting stone, causing her to wince and bite her tongue.

The rocky floor beneath her had been chiseled into a wide rectangle. She was on a stone staircase that seemed to grow from the side of the mountain. She could only guess that the stairs had been man-made as she scooted forward and peered past the edge. A few steps rose above her, but she had no interest in going up. Her gut told her she needed to go deeper into the mountain.

She regretted the loss of her boots as she peeked down the path. All she could see beyond the steps that unfolded below her was dark, empty space. She stood and steadied herself against the wall.

She stepped down onto the next rectangle and then stood still, listening for any sound rising up from below. Satisfied that her single step had not alerted anyone to her presence, she repeated the action.

# 35

# Kiami - Waiting Game

Kiami could see the entire valley below. The field within it was filled with wildflowers glowing with brightly colored butterflies that had come in search of sweet nectar. She headed toward it with the intention of finding a spot to sit where she could get a full view of the mountain peak crowned in its icy headdress.

Two days had passed, but she still hadn't given up hope that she would see a sign of Amanda from somewhere on the mountain that loomed above her. Today, the azure sky held faint wisps of stratus clouds, and she drank in the sunlight that rained down on her.

Guilt gnawed at the corner of her mind, but she pushed it down easily enough by telling herself that if she returned with no news of Amanda, they would be disappointed in her.

She found the right spot and lay down in the wildflowers, causing a cloud of bright wings to flutter up and away from her. She was enjoying the view. She could even tell where the river twisted up the mountainside; the sun reflected off the water, making it sparkle. The surrounding background of the landscape contained several of the mountains, but she only focused on one.

She yawned and stretched out, assuring herself that she would leave in a day or two, whether she saw any sign of Amanda or not.

# 36

# Amanda - The Unexpected

As she had moved further downward, the wall had begun to feel slick with damp clay. Wherever she touched it, it dried quickly onto her skin, dulling the sensation of the rocks that supported her. She didn't like it at all.

Amanda had stopped to pick the crusted clay from her fingertips when she heard voices below her. They sounded like whispers, but she knew it was just because she was so high above them.

She tiptoed along the edge of the step and peered over. As she leaned forward, a few loose rocks were brushed to the edge by her foot. She held her breath as the spray of dust and debris fell. She didn't hear them reach the floor.

Amanda stepped backward and pressed herself into the wall, still holding her breath. Her heart thundered in her chest as she lowered herself into a sitting position and breathed out.

She would need to get closer if she wanted to hear the conversation. She slid down to the next step and then the next, moving forward with caution each time. She wasn't sure how close she could get without alerting them to her presence. She was so engrossed in her thoughts as she slid down one step at a time that she gasped when a steady voice spoke from behind her.

"Lose it."

She turned her head to see someone standing over her. The voice had sounded soft and feminine, but a long-hooded cloak hid her body and face. She was gesturing to the staff that Amanda held in her hand.

She dropped it, watching as it bounced off the surface of the next few steps before it tipped sideways down over the edge and out of sight. She cursed herself for obeying without question, sure she could have taken on the woman if she had tried.

"Move."

This time she attempted to stand firm, but a familiar sensation invaded her muscles. It reminded her of the magic Jacob had used to make her limbs obey when he had kidnapped her.

She hated it.

When her feet hit the surface of the cave floor, the feeling evaporated and Amanda darted her head around the cavern.

There was a large, open area, making her suspect that the majority of the mountain was hollow. The air in the cave felt cool, even though she didn't see any holes for ventilation. Dark red clay pots were lined up against one of the cave walls. Several of them were cracked or shattered, and broken shards were scattered here and there around them.

There wasn't much in the way of furniture, knick-knacks, or things you would consider necessities to live in such a place, even though several people huddled together on the opposite side, whispering back and forth.

She returned her gaze to the woman. When she pushed her hood back from her face, Amanda couldn't believe what she was seeing. Her eyes grew wide in astonishment, but the tall blond woman didn't smile at her or offer up any explanation before she strode toward the group of people that watched her.

Amanda's face flushed and grew hot. For a moment she stood still, unsure of how to proceed. Feelings of confusion and doubt welled up inside her.

This was the woman that her father had fallen in love with all those years ago, and yet she showed no sign of acknowledging the fact, and for a moment Amanda second-guessed herself, thinking her imagination was running wild.

But her eyes held the same strange red hue as Amanda's own, and beyond that, she bore a striking resemblance to the woman in the photo her father had given her.

She remembered how she had always thought the reddened eyes in the photo were a flaw in the picture, but now it made more sense to her. It was like her own eyes were being reflected at her, but if Fatin saw the resemblance, she gave no indication.

A sudden sadness filled her; she had once longed to know her dad's enchantress, Fatin. She had wished she could hear her telling of how they met at his archeological site, curious if she had really and truly fallen for her father the way he suggested he had fallen for her. Or maybe, Amanda thought, she had just wanted to hear confirmation from her own mouth of the reasons she had sent her daughter away to grow up with only a father.

Then, after she had learned the truth of her heritage, the idea of meeting her had scared Amanda. She had thought her mom would be disappointed at having such a weak daughter when she had seemed so strong. It had to take strength to leave the ones you loved behind, didn't it?

Amanda clenched her fists at her side, now surer than ever that she wasn't wrong. If Fatin didn't want her as a daughter, she would not call her Mom, ever. Her stomach turned sour. Enraged, she called out to her, "How dare you just walk away from me."

The woman whipped around with such a quick movement that her long hair unfurled, fanning around her face. But as Amanda stared back into her eyes, she didn't see the anger she was expecting. They looked blank, numb. It was as if she had no feelings left to give, and Amanda pitied her. With the thought, a sour taste filled her mouth. Hadn't she, herself, been suppressing her own feelings since the loss of her father, her home, her friends? She couldn't help but wonder if she would have the same dead stare if she continued.

She unclenched her fists and glanced at the other people in the room. Apart from Fatin, they all had a sad, desperate look about them. She couldn't put her finger on it. She returned her gaze to her mother, who still stood, looking at her. "I know who you are, Fatin."

Her eyes looked cold as she responded, "It makes no difference to me or any of us." She glanced around at the others, raising her eyebrows in a challenging way. "Does it?"

They collectively looked down at the floor and shook their heads.

Overwhelmed, Amanda ignored the others as she walked up to Fatin, staring her dead in the eyes. "So I am nothing to you?"

The woman winced at her words but seemed to shake them off. "You were something once."

She reached a hand toward Amanda's face, cupping her chin, then let her arm drop as she turned away. "Your being here was all he needed to draw the others in." She shook her head. "We all agreed that when the time came... There is no point in being sentimental."

Amanda breathed out; she hadn't even realized she had been holding her breath. She wanted to slap Fatin, but she took a step back to examine the faces of the others.

Realizing she recognized one of the onlookers, she moved toward him, furrowing her eyebrows. "You're Justin's father. I have seen pictures of you. You didn't die in that crash with his mom."

The man averted his eyes. "I may as well have."

"Are you all..." Amanda stumbled over her thought, unsure of what to call them. She was certain parents of cursed children wasn't the right way to put it. If they were, why would they be held in the human realm?

Why would this be the best place for them to be imprisoned? Even as she thought of it, the words that Fatin had used clicked in her brain: it was so that she and the others would find them.

A lanky woman spoke up. "We tried, you know, to get away. Most of us did for a while; some of us at least managed to hide the children."

Fatin rushed toward them then, grabbing the woman by her robe. "He will be back any time. Watch what you say." The woman bowed her head and hurried to move as far from them as she could.

The others, who had been crowding toward her, were now also moving away. Only Justin's father remained. "You made it here, and the others will follow, just like he wanted. He will keep you. Just like he keeps us."

Amanda shook her head. "They have their own mission."

"Yes, but when they realize you aren't coming back, they will look for you. Kiami knows where you were headed. She will tell them when they ask." He looked up at her. "Even if she thinks it's dangerous."

Amanda shook her head. "She hates me."

"No, she doesn't."

Fatin reached for her hand, and she refused it. "She's not strong enough to stay away from you."

"Don't try to pretend you care about me. How do you know anything about Kiami?"

Fatin crossed her arms in front of herself. "I have seen through your eyes, just like you have seen through theirs. It's an affliction we share, except I only see through you. Not the others. I have ever since you were born."

Justin's father pushed his hair back from his face in a way that reminded Amanda of his son. He turned his eyes to Fatin. "You should have hidden your visions from him better. If you hadn't told him, he may not have known."

Fatin sneered, "It matters little. Jacob still would have found her. It wouldn't have changed anything."

He stepped closer to her, raising his voice. "Maybe it would have."

"Enough," was all she said, but it was all she needed to say. He backed up and moved away, as the others had.

It was clear to Amanda that Fatin was in charge here, at least when their captor wasn't present. She had so many questions for the others, but if this mysterious man was going to show up soon, she wanted her staff at hand. She moved around the length of the cavern before heading toward the stairs, searching for it.

She was careful not to step on the broken fragments of clay pottery scattered around the floor. Some of the pieces were stained a dark red, like the clay on her fingertips. Blankets, pillows, a large worn table, and several small stools were all pushed into one side of the cave. She couldn't imagine that these people had lived here so long. How could they? There was nothing here.

Fatin followed her. "There is no way out. The stairs go up into another small cave, but you won't find an exit."

Amanda turned to her, ready to ask about her staff, but as she opened her mouth to speak, she was interrupted by another voice.

It was the tone of the voice that made the hair on the back of her neck and her arms prickle. It set off instant alarm bells in her head. Amanda bolted for the first step on the staircase, but as her foot landed, the rock beneath it crumbled into dust.

She stumbled backward, her arms flailing behind her, but Fatin grabbed her shoulder to steady her, whispering in her ear, "You can't run from a celestial."

His eyes were otherworldly, a strange kaleidoscope of colors that didn't seem to stop moving. His visible skin shimmered as if he was covered in a fine powder made of stardust. But even with those attributes, the creature that had appeared in the cavern looked like flesh and blood to Amanda. He was bald, very light-skinned, and not much taller than she was.

He wore a brightly colored cloak that hung limply around his body.

She held her tongue, waiting for him to speak again, wondering if her mind had been playing tricks on her ears. He pointed one long finger at Fatin. "Chain her." Again, his voice boomed out, echoing around the cave.

Her mouth fell open, but she didn't fight it as Fatin grasped her hand and pulled her to the wall on the far right. She hadn't noticed the chains that dangled there. She closed her eyes as her mother clasped the shackles to her arms.

He approached them as she finished. "Go huddle back there with the others." Amanda frowned as she opened her eyes; he spoke to her like she was nothing.

In her state of shock, she had played with the idea that her mother had been willing to help him, especially with the way she had treated the other people here, but now it was very clear that she wasn't the only prisoner in this cave. They all were, her mother included.

"You." He looked her up and down. "You have been way too much trouble. But what can we expect from a half-blood monster?" His eyes became slits as he reached forward, moving his finger along her cheekbone.

He pulled his hand back as she opened her mouth to speak, as if he thought she would bite, and Amanda smiled at the idea of it. "Of course I agree that I can have monstrous tendencies. I am exactly what you made me be."

He lifted his face to the ceiling and bellowed, "Me? Hah. You know not what you speak of."

"Wasn't it you that set all of this into motion? Jacob kidnapping me, killing my father, destroying my home, torturing me, tormenting people I care about?" Amanda tugged at the chains, getting as close to him as possible.

"Did I set things into motion? Certainly. You were the first half-blood born, you know, so when Jacob saw an opportunity to bring your shadow magic out, I told him to take it.

"But I didn't advise Jacob on how to deal with you and your father. That was his own idea. He should have left his pet jinni at home. Especially when you stumbled onto that other one in the forest.

"He thought it was nothing more than a happy accident. He became greedy, and it made him gullible."

Jacob had believed it was a coincidence that she found and released Erol. The question was why didn't the celestial?

"The jinn have always been mischievous in nature and hold a soft spot for humans. They think these little games are helping. What they have failed to understand is that when my daughters created this planet and all of these magical races, they defied me."

He looked her in the eyes and cocked one of his brows. "You are a monster because of my daughters. I wouldn't have had to take such measures if they had followed my rules and done what they were told."

She thought of the creation myth and how it was said that the goddesses were supposed to each make their own small worlds but instead combined their efforts. "So that's it then? You want to teach your daughters a lesson? You are the one that should be destroyed."

"My daughters will be punished for what they did. We are playing the long game because it amuses me." He grinned from ear to ear. "After I discovered their treachery, I hid them in the Chaos realm and planted the seeds of revolt in the inhabitants' minds, seeds of hatred. They craved the guidance that my daughters failed to give. So it wasn't very hard to get their creations to fall into line after they saw how easily I could imprison them. In fact, many jumped at the chance to help me incorporate my plan."

"That's why the people of the Chaos realm are trying to destroy us?"

"Destroy you? They don't hate you. On the contrary, my dear, they worship you for the power you have to bring the barriers down. They even erected crude likenesses of you in the Chaos realm. Monuments of sorts."

His menacing smile grew. "They were just pushing you to cause a disturbance in the flimsy barrier my daughters created in order to hold this place together."

That wasn't right, she thought. Abaddon had wanted her dead. Something wasn't quite adding up. "I don't believe that all of your minions are following your rules."

"Ha. Well, he was under some misconception that you and your friends are stronger than we planned. But it's obvious he was wrong. I have you here, after all."

Was he saying that he orchestrated her parents meeting? Amanda couldn't keep the disgust from her face.

"Now you're getting it." He sneered down at her. "You and the others, your mixed heritage ruins the delicate balance my daughters created and throws the barriers out of sync."

He walked another slow circle around her. "It was far easier than I imagined to find potential parents for my project. How willing both humans and the magical races were to create a life just to earn favor with me. It is really very disturbing to think about."

A pang of disappointment shot through her at his words, but Amanda would not turn away from him. He would not force her to back down, as Jacob had. "Is this whole spectacle just for your amusement, or are you trying to appear more powerful than you are?" She raised her eyebrows at him as she felt his eyes burrow into her.

His mouth became a straight line. "I can destroy this place at any moment."

She kept her tone steady and applauded herself as she remained unwavering. "So then why haven't you?"

Amanda felt herself get pushed backward as he grabbed her hair and twisted it into his fist. "Your attitude has always gotten you into trouble. You won't feel so bold after you have spent a real amount of time down here."

She pushed her arm forward again as far as it would go, clawing at his face, but he didn't release her hair. He didn't even flinch. He lifted his free hand to his cheek, wiping at the bloody scratches that had appeared there.

"Fatin!" he growled. She rushed back into view with a small shard of clay pottery outstretched toward him. Amanda glanced in her direction and her heart leapt in her chest. She didn't look back at her. Instead, she trained her eyes on the celestial.

Amanda furrowed her brow and then shook the feeling off. It didn't matter, she told herself as he raised the sharp object toward her.

She lifted her mouth into a grin. "What? You're going to use that to put a gash on my pretty face?" At the moment, the idea of another mar on her physique didn't bother her in the slightest.

She locked her eyes back onto his and refused to break contact, even as she felt the sharp clay press against her cheek. She clenched her teeth but made sure her smile stayed put.

He released her hair just as she felt the warm blood oozing from the cut begin to trickle down her cheek.

She nodded at him as he backed up to inspect his handiwork. "Another scar for my collection."

"If you're trying to get under my skin, it won't work. I am going to go check on my daughters. If not for you and your friends being given the gemstones, they would have lost all confidence and washed their hands of this place long ago. You see, you using the stones has worked in my favor anyway. I want to let them know I have you and that they have no hope of saving this world."

"I don't believe you. If there was no hope, you wouldn't be here wasting your time now."

"My dear child, no matter how you have tried to change things, the ending will always be the same. I will win and they will lose, right along with you."

"I am not scared of you." Amanda called to her dark magic. She could feel it inching its way to the surface. The power wasn't as strong as it could have been if she had her staff, but she focused on him just the same.

As the cave shuddered with her power, he raised a hand toward her, a smile stretching across his face. The shadowy tendrils of her dark magic began to appear as if they were being pulled from her body by his powers.

"Stop, or I will direct your magic at them," he said, unmoving.

She knew he was referring to the huddled group of captives at the other end of the room. Had they really been willing to go along with his plan, as he had suggested? She stopped pushing but didn't look away from him.

"You can't hurt me, Amanda. Failure is your only option." He sneered, "Why do you think Abaddon and his minions have not been afraid to approach you and your companions? Because they know I will protect them. They have always known that even if you and your companions ended their lives, they would still be getting what they want, the thing they have worked for through their whole existence."

"The others will come." She spat the words out forcefully, as if they could damage him in some way.

"Oh, I am counting on it." His eyes shone with excitement. "The ones you haven't already burned your bridges with, anyway. And the ones that you have, well, I have been making sure that none of them have a safe place to go back to. So eventually they will find their way here, and one by one they will be collected. The barriers will crack, and the world will be thrust into confusion. Wars will erupt between the humanoids, and mayhem will take hold."

"Sounds exciting." Amanda breathed the words out.

"It will be, because then I will release my daughters so that they can watch what they built fall apart."

Amanda pressed her teeth together as she held on to her smile. "Well, by all means then go. Don't let me get in the way of good parenting."

Her mother was the first to speak after the celestial disappeared, "Stupid girl. Why would you act like that toward a celestial?" As she walked toward Amanda, her daughter saw sadness behind her eyes for the first time.

If the celestial was a literal being and the goddesses were imprisoned in the Chaos realm, where did that leave her and the others? He had clearly stated he was going to go see them. She wanted to understand. "Were you in on this from the start, like he said?"

Fatin shifted her eyes over the other prisoners. "In a way."

"You would condemn an entire planet so that he can teach his daughters a lesson?"

Fatin reached out and grabbed her chin, as if she was examining her wound. "Amanda, you cannot tell a celestial no."

Amanda couldn't keep the strained sound from entering her voice as she spoke. "So you didn't care about my father?"

Fatin released her chin. "I did. It's more complicated than that. I knew I couldn't hide, and I thought maybe your father could keep you safe... But I was wrong. We all were. We just infuriated him."

"He may be a celestial, as you call it, but he is flesh. He bleeds."

Fatin took a step back. "He is powerful; he knows everything."

Amanda shook her head and felt a twinge in her neck from the strain of her shackled position. "He is not omniscient. He just tries to make it seem like he is. "

"But he has ways of knowing everything."

*Not everything,* Amanda thought, but she bit her tongue. He was good at pushing people around on the chessboard, sure. But if he really controlled everything that was going on, why would he bother trying to collect and capture them?

Fatin placed a hand on her hip. "We were like trapped goldfish, swimming in circles in his aquarium. It's very hard to hide things from a celestial being, Amanda. We did the best we could."

Justin's father kept his voice low and steady as he approached. "He didn't know about the gemstones. They could do what we failed to do. If they can work together."

Fatin turned her eyes in his direction. "There is only one way she can escape and stop the others from coming here."

He lifted a hand and placed it on her shoulder. "Fatin, it must be done."

"What must be done?" Amanda blurted.

A sadness had filled Fatin's eyes, and the sternness returned to her voice as she responded, "You now know he is planning on using us to control the others like you. I think you already have an idea of what must be done."

Amanda looked at the floor, ashamed. She had an inkling of what her mother was insinuating, but she needed to find out if there was another way. "I don't understand. I am trapped here just like you. What am I supposed to do about it?"

Her mother's sadness seemed to turn to anger. Her voice rose several octaves. "You don't understand?"

Amanda let her chin drop down toward her chest, and she swallowed hard. She could hear Fatin breathing in and out in the same slow deliberate way she had been taught.

When Fatin spoke again, her voice was softer. "Sometimes you have to push people over the edge to get them to do what they need to do."

Amanda looked back up at Fatin, keeping her expression blank. She needed more information.

Justin's father removed his hand from her shoulder and dropped his arm at his side. "Fatin. We must tell Amanda what we know. There is no reason to be afraid of the repercussions anymore."

Fatin shook her head. "The universe is more than she can understand, and she is not equipped."

"Then we keep it simple. She knows the myth of creation already. She has hinted as much."

Fatin turned to face him. "It's really over for us?

"Our chance to make a difference passed by long ago. Parents make sacrifices for their children. It is the way it has always been."

Fatin hung her head as he continued. "The longer she is here, the weaker she will become."

What were they were insinuating she was capable of? Amanda couldn't take the back-and-forth between them. It was irritating. Did they want her to escape and leave them here to be punished? If she somehow managed it and the others caught wind of their parents' situation, they would still come to save them.

She wanted to get the conversation back on track. *Maybe there was another way*, she thought.

"Does your great celestial have a name?"

"If he does, we don't know it," the jinni offered.

Amanda shot him a half smile. "Please, Fatin. Explain what you know. I need to understand."

Her mother let out a huff before her eyes darted around, as if she was inspecting for spies of some sort. "Think of the myth. And hear me. I won't repeat what I am going to say."

Perhaps, Amanda thought, she didn't trust the other captives. Then she remembered the eyes in the tree she had encountered back at the town. She supposed magic of that particular sort could be used in many places and would be fairly hard to detect.

Fatin moved closer to Amanda and stared hard at her. "When the celestial devised his plan, he made sure that each magical being was paired with a human, because he believed that in doing so, there would be no way the children could ever be as powerful as him. He was right. You are not."

She paused and looked up at the jinni before locking her eyes back onto Amanda and continuing. "When Erol gave you the black diamond, it changed things."

Amanda shook her head. "The gemstones make the fluctuations in the barriers worse."

Fatin nodded. "Yes, but they also make you more powerful. Not enough that you could stop the celestial singlehanded, mind you, but enough for him to worry that if you all combined your abilities, you would be able to."

"And that's why he seems to hold so much disdain for the jinn? Because they pushed us together?"

Justin's father explained, "He thinks it was the jinn that started the whole thing. Placed Erol's prison where you could find it, everything."

"They didn't?"

"No." He shook his head. "The jinn believed that someone else saw what the gift did for you and decided to intervene by seeing that the gems found their way to each of you."

"Shh," Fatin scolded.

"Yes, Fatin, I know. The walls have ears. Still, even though there is no hope, she should know that someone, somewhere, has been looking out for her."

It was so much to take in, Amanda knew she had a confused look on her face, but she couldn't shake it. They were talking in circles. If they really thought there was no hope, why would they bother explaining all this? And then it dawned on her. When she only had a small idea of what her mother wanted her to do, it hadn't bothered her as much, but now that she was sure, it made her stomach turn. Fatin was implying that the only way to defeat the celestial was for herself and the offspring like her to all come together as one, and if she stayed in the cave or let the parents remain trapped here, all hope of saving the planet would be gone. She closed her eyes and took in a deep breath.

When she opened them, she could see that the other hostages had crowded around her, and she peered up into their faces. They scowled at her, but in contradiction, their eyes seemed to shimmer with a shared excitement that they were trying to keep hidden just beneath the surface. They wanted her to do it.

One of the other hostages looked up into her eyes with a frown, but somehow her expression seemed to exude hope. "It is a pity you hadn't come close to the end of the journey before you were captured. You would have had to find his daughters as well as joining the others. It could have been your only chance." The amethyst speckles in her eyes shone so bright, Amanda stared.

"What's your name?"

She looked around as if asking permission, and when no one protested she answered, "Lillian, but please don't tell her. These humans couldn't have children, and I thought..."

"Shhh," Fatin hissed. "Don't make it worse. Stick to your name." She stressed the word *your*, and Amanda realized that Fatin didn't want them saying certain things. She was worried about information falling into the celestial's hands.

Amanda nodded at Lillian; she understood. She didn't want Emily knowing that she had been left with another family for protection. It hadn't turned out how her actual parents had thought it would.

Justin's father reached forward and put an arm around Lillian's shoulder as he looked up at Amanda. "Amal."

She offered him a smile, but had a hard time holding it. Thoughts of how much Justin seemed to dislike her already permeated her mind. If she did what they wanted, she would never hope to gain his trust.

As if he could hear her thoughts, he spoke again. "The jinn and my child already believe I am gone. The damage was done long ago."

They continued to watch her as if pleading with her to do what they were suggesting. Amanda closed her eyes again. This time, when she gulped, the noise it seemed to echo in her head. She let her chin drop onto her chest.

There were three others: two men and a woman. She could only guess what children they were linked to. Perhaps ones she hadn't even met yet. She didn't want to know. She was relieved when they didn't offer their names.

At least Kiami was different. As far as Amanda knew, her guardian Jacqueline was still in the jinni realm. She didn't have parents in that sense of the word, unless Bloise was lying, which she doubted. He had said the goddesses created her and hinted that they knew that the celestial was coming.

They had known that if someone could wield the stone that represented their realm, there would be a chance. Without someone, they knew they wouldn't be able to save their world. They had put a part of themselves into Kiami and then put her away for safekeeping.

She recognized Fatin's voice whispering in her ear, "Believe me when I say we can't ever leave here."

Was she insinuating that Amanda could? It was happening again. She was being asked to make a choice she didn't want to make. But was it really a choice? She struggled with her thoughts.

Could she let the others come here one by one and die, or worse? It was why Bloise had insisted she come alone. He knew the others wouldn't be able to see it through.

She wished she could cry, but it was like she had no tears left to give.

She feigned sleep. She couldn't listen to anymore right now.

# 37

# Emily - Powerless

As the morning shifted into afternoon, Emily had just about given up on waiting for Justin to return.

In her restless state, she had tried to keep herself busy by cleaning her bedroom.

The process didn't take long to accomplish in her small space, so when she reemerged, she tackled the sink that was full of dirty dishes. After that, she set out to erase the thin layer of dust that had settled over the unused surfaces throughout the house.

She saved Nina's curio cabinet for last. The wooden piece of furniture was designed to fit snugly in the corner, and it looked right at home in the dining area.

It wasn't something she would touch on an average day. Not because the trinkets inside looked old or expensive. On the contrary, the collection of white porcelain bells and snow globes displayed on its shelves seemed pretty average. Yet the idea of opening the windowed doors to adjust them felt like an invasion of Nina's personal space.

Instead, she stood up on her toes, holding the cloth out in front of her, and made a quick swipe at the top to clear it of accumulated dust.

She was taken a bit by surprise when an object much larger than the expected spray of particles flew past her head.

She lowered her heels to the ground and moved to find the object, hoping whatever it was hadn't been damaged in the fall.

It didn't take long for her to spot the necklace on the floor. Curious, she lifted it up by the chain and studied the transparent gem with her eyes. It twisted around with the movement of her fingertips as it hung there, shimmering a silvery blue from within as it caught the light from the windows.

This was Kiami's moonstone.

Without much thought, she carried the piece of jewelry outstretched in front of her upstairs to add it to the backpack with Etzion's, Justin's, and her own. Once the gem was out of sight, she resumed the household chores.

With all the work they had been doing at Justin's, until now, she hadn't noticed that they had allowed things here to fall by the wayside.

As she moved from room to room sweeping and tidying, life seemed almost normal. Once she finished fluffing and straightening everything she could think of, she plopped down onto a chair.

She stayed there until the last rays of the late afternoon sun fell slanting through the window, wrestling with the idea of going to look for Justin.

She had just made up her mind to leave as he walked in through the front door with a deep frown plastered on his face.

"Are you ready to leave, or do you think we should skip going?" he asked listlessly.

Irritated, Emily lifted her arms above her head in shocked exasperation. "Skip it? I have been waiting here all day."

He fidgeted as he answered, pulling at his collar as if it was constricting his air flow. "Sorry. I got a little sidetracked wandering around town. I miss Cherry, Gemma, and, well, everyone."

She felt her cheeks heat up as she lowered her arms at her side; she hadn't meant to embarrass him.

"Still no changes, huh?"

He shook his head. "Are you ready to go?"

"Almost."

She snatched the photo up from where she had left it on the desk and held out in front of her.

"Take this while I go up and grab my backpack."

He wrinkled his brow as he accepted it. "What do you need this for?"

"For Etzion. I will explain on the way."

Emily smiled as bounded back up the stairs; her spirits had lifted somewhat since the morning. She had the wisps to thank for that.

Maybe, she reasoned, a meaningful task would help to suppress Justin's disappointment as well.

By the time Emily had explained her encounter with the wisps and how she had happened upon Kiami's hidden necklace, they were pulling up to the dirt path that led to Justin's home.

"Did you put it back?"

"No. I have it here," she said as she lifted the backpack up from the floor. "Should I have?"

Justin shrugged. "I don't see why Kiami would care. You are keeping them safe."

As she moved to open her car door, he reached over to stop her. "Wait here."

He popped his door open and jumped out. The door swung shut with a bang as he raced around the front of the vehicle to open hers.

Emily rolled her eyes at him as he bowed to her and offered his hand. "My lady."

She accepted, snickering. She was happy to see the gloom had lifted from him, even if it was only temporary.

Emily grabbed the backpack with her free hand as he helped her up from her seat.

She released his hand and dropped the bag onto the ground beside her before offering him a curtsy. "Thank you."

By the time Emily had registered the hunched figured running at them, she knew she only had seconds to react.

The first thing that popped into her head was that the stones were dangerous, but she pushed it aside. Amanda would want answers.

She reached out to clasp on to Justin's arm.

She was careful to kept her voice low and controlled. "Don't do anything."

Emily felt his pulse quicken as he looked at her with wide eyes and then at the filthy man that was almost on them.

"Don't." She held firm as the man came up beside them.

Without stopping, he bent down and grabbed for the strap of the bag, dragging it with him as he continued.

He came to a halt in the center of the yard, and then he dropped down to his knees.

Emily let go of Justin and began walking in the man's direction. She was going to find out once and for all who had been watching from the woods.

She heard Justin's footfalls as he hurried to follow behind her. "What are you doing?"

"We are going to find out who this is, right now."

The man didn't acknowledge them as they approached. He had unzipped the bag and tipped it upside down, dumping the contents in front of him.

He reached out toward the stones and Emily called out, "Jacob."

The man's hand stopped and hovered where it was.

"You know if you pick those up, it won't be pleasant." She paused just a few feet in front of him and crossed her arms over her chest.

The man's gray, matted hair hung over his eyes, concealing them. "Don't care." He lifted his other hand and stretched it forward, scooping all four gems up at once.

Emily took a step backward and tried again. "Jacob, stop before it's too late."

He tilted his head back and opened his eyes wide, revealing a weather-worn face twisted in agony. The muscles in his hands flexed as he clutched the stones tighter.

"Not him anymore." The words came out in a wheeze, as if he the air was being squeezed from him.

He gritted his teeth as smoke began to rise up from between his knuckles.

She felt Justin's firm grip as he clasped his hand on her shoulder. "Em?"

Emily pulled her eyes away and refocused on Justin. "What do we do?"

"This was your idea."

"I didn't have much time to think it through," she squeaked.

A foul, acidic smell reached her noise, and she turned her eyes back to Jacob. His entire body was enveloped in a glowing field of energy.

A puddle of oil like liquid surrounded his feet. The fluid substance was streaming down his arms and legs, like the wax of a lighted candle.

"He's melting," Justin croaked.

Emily turned away and squeezed her eyes shut.

Justin tugged at her, trying to move her away, but she couldn't let him.

When he gave up, she allowed her shoulders to slump and hung her head. Hot tears began to roll down her cheeks. She knew Jacob had done terrible things, but that didn't matter to her.

She had caused this by making it easy for him to take the bag.

She felt the weight of Justin's hand lift from her shoulder. It was replaced by the light touch of his index finger as he tilted her chin up.

"It's over, Em."

She expected to see anger when she opened her eyes and looked into his. Instead she saw only concern. Her voice cracked as she addressed him. "I didn't mean for this to happen."

He released her chin and gently brushed one of her curls away from her face. "I know."

She wrung her hands as she explained, "I was trying to be like Kiami and Amanda. They always seem to act so fast."

Justin raised an eyebrow at her, causing lines to appear on his forehead. "Why are you trying to be like them?"

"Amanda keeps pushing me to lead."

He reached for her hands and gripped them. "If she is pushing you to lead, it's not because she wants you to act like her."

# 38

## Amanda - Dream on

The celestial may not have looked angry when he left, but when he returned, he was fuming.

"Where is your gem? Are you using it somehow to block us from seeing the village?"

She released a sigh. She was relieved to hear that Justin had managed to stop the prying eyes. "What are you going on about?"

"Don't be coy, Amanda. Nothing you can do will stop me. This world will be destroyed."

Her eyes were trained on the floor. Her neck and shoulders were throbbing from the strain of the position she had been left in. "I have no idea how the others stopped your prying eyes, but even if I did, I wouldn't help you. I refuse."

"Your stone! Where is it?"

"I don't know. I seem to have misplaced it."

"You are lying!"

Amanda gave her head a shake. She wished she wasn't.

"If you can do what you say, well, I certainly won't make it any easier for you." She raised her head and looked him in the eyes. "Until my last breath and after, I will haunt you for all eternity."

He lifted one side of his mouth in a sneer and looked her up and down. "You will regret being so disrespectful to me."

"Let me down. I need a fight. I guarantee that only one of us will make it out alive."

"Fatin." He spun away from her as he bellowed his question. "What's the best way to punish you both?"

"You can't," Fatin breathed as she approached. It was the first time Amanda had ever heard her say anything back to him. Amanda didn't miss the way she flinched at the look he shot her.

"I can do whatever I want. I brought those women into this universe, and they created you and this world, so by proxy, you are all mine."

He turned back to Amanda, and she smiled up at him. "If everything that you say is true, then you must have expected me to be this way. After all, according to what you are saying, you created us, in a way." She stretched her smile as wide as she could. The movement hurt, but it was worth it to see the look on his face. "Besides, the things you put into motion molded us into being the way we are. And we are, make no mistake, a force that you can't control, try as you may."

Amanda ignored the erratic hammering of her heart as his expression changed. His eyes narrowed, and the irises seemed to vanish altogether. His stance became rigid. Even his focus seemed to shift to somewhere behind her, as if he couldn't bear to look at her any longer.

In that moment, she knew she'd crossed some invisible line, offended him beyond reconciliation, but she pushed again. "This is not your world, and you can't have it. You are pathetic."

He was seething. His pale skin had begun to radiate a bright red, even at the tops of his flat, rounded ears. He crinkled his nose in disgust and opened his cloak. He pulled out a long metal sword, and she could see her face reflected on its shiny silver surface. She knew he was just taunting her with it.

She slitted her eyes at him. "If you're a god, why can I hear your heartbeat drumming inside your chest?"

His eyes shifted back in her direction. The sword glowed a bright orange as he lifted it up and brought it back down. It happened so fast that at first she felt nothing apart from her body shifting sideways and hitting the cave wall. One of the shackles had been released.

It took time for the realization of what had happened to sink in. He had sliced through her arm.

Screams reverberated from the far wall, echoing through the cave in the same way the celestial's voice did. Amanda looked at her shoulder as her knees gave out beneath her, the wrist that remained shackled burned from supporting all of her weight.

No blood spurted from the empty space where the arm had been; charred flesh and cloth were all that remained below her shoulder. Small tendrils of smoke emanated there, reminding her in a way of her own shadow magic. The seconds ticked by, as if her brain was having trouble processing what it was seeing.

A full minute had to have passed before it hit. Excruciating pain like she had never felt rushed through her in a torrent. Delirious from the shock, she felt her mouth open and her throat contort as screams tore their way out.

She heard the celestial call for someone to get her down, and she heard the onlookers' cries become muffled. She felt herself being lifted and then laid flat, but still she screamed. Her throat was raw and her voice had become hoarse from the effort.

She welcomed the darkness as it began to envelop her.

Amanda wasn't aware of how she had arrived in the dream realm. Had she brought herself there, or had someone helped her? She wasn't sure. Her first memory upon the darkness lifting had been that of the golden apples that grew on the tree there. She only prayed that she could find some now.

Dull pain radiated from her shoulder even here. She looked at the wound but didn't reach up to touch it. Someone had slathered orange goop over the burned flesh. She could only imagine what the substance was. She assumed it was for healing and discomfort.

She had thought the celestial might kill her, but she never imagined he would do something like this. She turned herself around in the field, scanning it for the tree that she had walked to so many times before. When she saw the silhouette of its outline, she focused on it, pulling herself closer.

As she moved toward it, the sight of the tree's barren branches brought her to her knees at its base. A choked cry escaped her swollen throat. She leaned forward and rested her forehead awkwardly against the bark.

Even though she knew the others wouldn't be coming to her aid, she had felt invincible when she was speaking to the celestial. She realized now that she had gone too far. She touched the bark with her hand and ran her fingers down it as if it were a living breathing creature that she was petting. "I'm sorry," she whispered. "So sorry."

The breeze kicked up, and a moan sounded from above her. She thought it was just the wind moving through the branches, but it startled her upright. She stood still, searching the treetop, but she didn't see anything besides sky beyond its branches.

She averted her eyes to the ground as she felt something slender move against her leg. Several snapped and broken-off branches wiggled in the dirt around her, moving like snakes in the grass.

She didn't bother to push them away as they began to move up her calf and thigh. Instead, she placed her forehead back against the tree and closed her eyes, resigning herself to her fate.

She whispered so low she could barely hear her own voice, "Let it be what it must."

Glad that she was too tired even to try to scream, she could feel them wriggle into the goop that had been plastered over her wound, inserting themselves into her flesh and beneath it. She hadn't thought her pain could get any worse than when the celestial had severed her arm, but now it itched, burned, and tingled all at the same time.

And then the sensation moved past where she knew the wound to be, farther down her missing arm. The throbbing pain returned but began to be replaced by a dull heat that radiated from the wound.

She felt a fist clench. Her fist. It was followed by a feeling similar to the rush of blood into a sleeping limb. When the strange sensations abated, she pushed herself back up to inspect the damage.

It felt like her arm, but it looked off, rougher, almost like it had a thin layer of bark applied to it. She flexed the muscles and touched the wooden extremity with her fleshy fingers. It didn't feel rough, like wood.

It was somewhere in between flesh and plant. She pinched the surface. She felt the squeeze, but it seemed duller than usual. She wiggled the fingers and frowned. They moved like normal, but they weren't hers.

It felt wrong.

Her stomach flopped. What she felt at seeing the new limb wasn't joy.

She couldn't help feeling like she was being pulled in two directions at once. On one side of her, the opposition would stop at nothing to make her want to give up, and the other side wouldn't let her even if she needed to.

She was trapped with no way out.

She sensed herself being pulled away from the dream realm, and she was furious.

# 39

# Amanda - Collapse

When Amanda opened her eyes, she was lying on the rough cave floor. She had been positioned on her side with her face only a few inches from a stone wall. A blanket had been thrown over her, and its scratchy texture reminded her of the one her rescuer had draped her with before leaving her in the small outer cave. For a moment she imagined that her descent toward the interior of the mountain and the things that followed had all been a dream brought on by her near drowning.

She moved her arms under the material to hug herself. As the soft flesh from her normal hand met the shoulder of her new arm, she trembled beneath the blanket. It had all happened.

The rage she had felt when she was being pulled from the dream realm trickled back in as whispers from across the room tickled at her ears. Her own mother, Justin's father, and the other parents had all played a part in this.

She pushed herself up into a sitting position, making sure that the blanket covered her new arm as she moved to face the other captives.

She examined their faces as they looked back at her, expecting her to speak. Her rage and disgust at what they had done wasn't enough. In fact, letting them witness the celestial get what he wanted felt like the punishment they deserved. She needed courage to do what they asked.

She opened her mouth and began speaking to herself at a volume she knew only she would be able to understand. "I was raised blind. Lost in the shadows of what I was until I chose to find out the truth. I learned a power was always in me, biding its time."

Someone murmured, "What's that?"

"She is babbling."

The onlookers began to move closer as they strained to understand her.

She recognized Amal's voice as it carried over the others. "On the contrary, I think she knows exactly what she is saying."

She nodded. "I'm ready. I am giving the unknown another chance."

She had expected Fatin to be the one to produce her missing staff, but it was Justin's father that approached her. "This is yours."

She couldn't say she was disappointed. She knew someone had hidden it from the celestial and from herself, although she wasn't sure how. She assumed it was done as a precaution so that she wouldn't hand it over to him. She had only hoped it was her mother who had hidden it.

She accepted her staff with her unharmed arm and held it on her lap. As Fatin stepped forward, Amanda let the blanket fall from her shoulder. "I'm saving myself to save them. As you suggested. I hope that you are not having doubts. It's too late to change my mind."

"What have you done to yourself?"

"Like you, I did nothing. It was done to me. Everything comes with a price, but this time I won't be the one to pay it." She looked around the cave. "You, all of you, just stood there."

She locked her eyes back onto Fatin's. "I guess you felt I needed that push you were talking about."

Fatin whispered, "Our dignity has been stripped away long ago."

"We used to have purpose," someone else offered.

"You still do," Amanda explained. "It is unfortunate. They will come looking for you, and he will have them." She looked at Amal. "I realized you were right. Even if I escape, it won't stop them from coming to find you. The draw for answers from their parents is too strong."

The other four moved closer. "Now that I know my purpose, I can relieve you of yours." She found her mother's eyes, "But first, I have to thank you. For showing me why you wanted me. I was born to hurt, destroy, and nothing more."

"Your father didn't know until after you were born," Fatin offered.

Amanda shrugged. "He could have told me the truth. He should have prepared me better."

Fatin didn't bother to argue as Amanda leapt to her feet.

If she didn't move fast, she would lose her nerve.

The rage she felt toward them was fleeting. She didn't just hate them - she pitied them as well. They were victims of the celestial, as much as she was.

At the thought of him, fresh hatred burned within her. She could almost feel it rippling beneath her skin. "Where is he?" Her newly hardened leaf-like nails dug into the wood of her staff.

They stepped back as one. "Gone. We don't know where."

She gave a nod. "I expected as much. The show must go on. Are you ready?"

Amanda didn't wait for them to respond. She raised her staff and let the dark magic release from her in waves like she had never felt before.

She was almost blinded by the intensity as the mountain shook, beginning to crumble around her. It was fueled by her uncontrolled anger, she knew, but right now that was all she could allow herself to feel. She ground her teeth as her shadow magic encircled her, protecting her from the debris that cascaded everywhere.

Despite the fact that Amal had insisted Kiami didn't hate her, Amanda couldn't help but suspect that the celestial had been right when he said no one would want her to return, especially if they knew what she had done to escape, regardless of the circumstances.

She breathed in deeply as her shadow magic lifted her from the rubble. A long time ago, she had promised herself that she would see this through to the end, and she intended to keep that promise.

Before she could even attempt to join the others and finish this, she needed to find the goddesses and release them.

She was going to use her gem to get to the Chaos realm. The consequences of utilizing it wouldn't matter in the end, if the world was destroyed anyway.

In the meantime, she realized, she would miss Kiami, Emily, and even Justin.

# 40

# Kiami - Shaken

At first Kiami couldn't move; her brain was unable to make sense of the input from her ears and feet. The vibrations she felt were coming from below her, and she knew they were a gentle warning of what was about to happen.

She needed to move, but her feet felt glued to the ground as her teeth locked together and dread settled over her features. Her heart began beating so loud that she swore she could hear the echo in her brain. She could feel the hairs on the back of her neck bristling, just as the ground rippled beneath her, making her flounder. She stumbled forward and the rumbling increased, sounding like thunder in her ears.

Ahead of her she could see snow, land, and rocks sliding down the side of the mountain in a rush. The debris from the peaks was moving toward the lower areas of the mountainside, where the rugs of green and yellow trees that stretched out around its base were about to be scarfed up.

She called to her magic. She needed to change now.

When her transformation started, she could hear the first trees creak and groan as they were pushed over by the weight, their roots ripped up from the mountainside. They thudded to the ground.

She lifted her wings and flew toward the peak as fast as she could, but the upper portions were crumbling in on themselves. She didn't dare to swoop down for a closer look. It would be too dangerous.

She could only watch as the unstable mountain collapsed below her. Eerie, muffled noises sounded from beneath her, but even with her exceptional hearing, they were such faint sounds that she couldn't determine if they were screams or just the ground itself crying out in protest as the mass disintegrated.

When the movement stopped and the dust settled, Kiami landed in the mound of dirt and plants. She couldn't help but wonder if this was the sign she had been waiting for. She had, after all, witnessed the capabilities of Amanda's magic first-hand. There was no doubt in her mind that it was a possibility.

Her hands began to tremble; the static feel in the air was unmistakable. It was heavy with a familiar magic. Although she couldn't detect any of the tendrils of shadowy smoke she had seen in the past, she knew this wasn't a natural quake.

Kiami hoped that the cries she had heard were nothing more than her imagination. Trying to dig deep enough with her bare hands to know for sure would be a hopeless task, she understood that. But the thought that people could have been trapped under tons of rubble was even more disheartening. She chewed at her nails. No one could have survived the fall unless they were well prepared. She would be looking for mangled and dusty corpses.

She began to descend the mound a few steps at a time, studying the debris for clues as to what had happened beyond Amanda using her magic. If she had done this, there had to be a good reason, Kiami reassured herself.

About midway down the hill, she spotted a few of the smoky coils she had seen at Justin's, but they led nowhere this time. She had gotten her wish.

Kiami bit at her nails again as she contemplated what it could mean.

She supposed the trails could have faded away already, but it seemed to her that the wispy smoke closest to the ground would have dispersed first. Unless, she thought, pulling her finger away from her teeth, Amanda had left the human realm altogether.

The glimmer of something half buried in the ground caught her eye, and she moved toward it. When she leaned down, muddy water welled up into the heels of the imprints her feet made in the dirt. She dug around the piece of metal until she could remove it from the mud and clay blend. She wasn't sure what the tool was for. It was a long, slender, cylindrical shape, only about an inch thick, with a rough ball attached at one end.

Another glint caught her eye along the ground, and she stood back up and squinted as she studied the surrounding area. Mixed in with the wreckage of rocks, ground, and roots were peculiar pieces of inorganic material the likes of which she had never seen. She found several long pieces of the same metal substance, but in different shapes and sizes scattered here and there.

A few were small and round, and when she ventured to inspect them closer, the material seemed more consistent with plastic than metal. Kiami collected several of the smaller bits and placed them inside the hood of her cloak, using the strings to cinch it closed.

She wanted to show the others when she returned. She expected that Justin would have some ideas about what was in the mountain from viewing them.

As she descended, clumps of red fur were scattered, lying in the ruins of what was once a lush forest. The trees were knocked down in all directions, the leaves still bright green with life, and roots were still attached at the bases as if yanked from the ground during a child's tantrum.

As she crept deeper into the woods that were no longer woods, she heard no creatures rustling. Scared, they must have fled and made it away and had not yet felt safe to return and inspect the damage. Were they safe? Was she?

Her eyes darted around as worry trickled in. If Amanda had caused this devastation, there had to have been something terrible inside that mountain. She dropped the cloak she had been clutching in her hand and concentrated on making one of her talons appear.

She flinched at the pain and held her breath until it was over. It would only take a second to tear the extra material away from the hood, then she could secure the satchel she had created around her ankle and finish the change.

Her unease grew with each second that passed. She knew she wouldn't feel relief until she was high above the peaks of the surrounding mountains and on her way back to Emily and Justin.

# 41

# Emily - Mission Statement

On the morning that Kiami returned, Emily had been sitting on the front porch of the house, listening with her eyes closed to the almost absolute silence, feeling nothing but the warmth of the early morning sunrise on her face as she waited for Justin to return from town.

The last few days had passed as if thousands of camera frames were shown just one at a time, and with each day gone, she felt more hollow inside.

She yearned for someone beside him to talk to about the history of three, Jacob, or even the picture that now hung on the wall of Justin's guest room.

She was isolated and lonely. She knew that this kind of solitude brought peace to some, but for her it was like a reminder of the past, only worse.

Emily, who had been used to being alone, had become accustomed to the friendly town banter, despite the fact that she wasn't always feeling sociable.

It wasn't just being alone – it was the silence that comes with real true isolation, she thought.

Even when she had been locked in her room at night by her parents, there were always things going on. Cars moving down the street, neighbors greeting one another, her parents going in and out.

She wanted to move on, she wanted it to be over.

When Kiami had emerged, mumbling, from around the side of the house, she had needed to stop herself from jumping up and embracing her.

In general, Kiami was the optimist and the one that calmed others down, but Emily had noticed the evident fear in her eyes.

Something was wrong. Even at a distance, Emily could see that she was shaking from head to toe. She clutched a ragged cloth to her chest. It appeared as though she had torn a piece from her cloak to create a makeshift bag.

Emily glanced down the road for any sign of Justin.

After the battle with the wolves, Kiami had been in a state of shock, but this was different. Emily wasn't sure if she could bring her back from her rattled state alone. She wasn't even sure that Kiami had registered her sitting there in plain sight, but she had to try.

"Kiami."

Startled by the sound of her voice, Kiami spun in her direction. Her fingers twitched, wrapping even more tightly around the bag.

"Why don't you sit here." Emily made slow movements as she stood and offered the cushioned sun chair to her friend.

Kiami closed her eyes and breathed out. A sigh of relief, Emily imagined.

When she opened her eyes again, she took measured steps toward the chair and then plopped down into it, letting her rigid shoulders fall to a more relaxed position. She left one hand over the bag, her fingers still gripping the top.

As Emily stood watching her, she tried to keep the concern from spreading across her features. Kiami would speak when she was ready, and Emily wasn't going to push her. She hoped Justin would show up soon.

The minutes ticked by like hours before Kiami opened her mouth.

"I never knew that time could be so..." she paused, and sat forward with a start, "so much like water?"

Her brow furrowed as she explained. "It can pass by as a single drop, rush by in a blink, or freeze solid."

Emily kneeled down beside her and reached for her free hand. "You're wrong. It's not exactly like water. Water can be manipulated. We can't stop time, reverse it, or slow it down."

Kiami's face went blank as she stared at her.

"What happened, Kiami?"

"So many things." She leaned back into the chair. "I know that I said the mountain was dangerous, but it was so serene, so majestic. It was easy to forget while I was waiting for her. I never imagined how right I was, and now it's gone. Just like that."

Emily tilted her head. "What do you mean, gone?"

"There was a terrible rumble from deep in the belly of the ground. For a moment, I couldn't bring myself to leave my spot. Then the earth began to move as if it were a wave on the sea, as the mountain, the very mountain that I knew Amanda had been exploring, began to crumble in and collapse into its own foundation."

"Is that why you are so frightened?" Emily bit at her lip in nervous anticipation.

"It wasn't what Amanda had done that scared me - it was the idea of why she did it. Do you know what I mean?" Kiami's eyes burrowed into her own. "What was she saving herself, and possibly us from?"

Emily's eyes widened in disbelief as she withdrew her hand. "Are you saying Amanda caused the mountain to collapse?"

She nodded solemnly. "I waited for the dust to settle. Amanda was nowhere to be seen. Only traces of her magic remained."

Emily's mind reeled with the information, questions sprouting: *Do we assume that she is dead? Do we continue? Could she have gotten out before it collapsed?*

As if Kiami understood her silence, she spoke again. "She's not dead; I would know. We would know."

Emily nodded. The bond they all shared from the beginning had been developing into something more since they had met face to face. In fact, when Kiami and Amanda left, she felt as if something was missing.

Kiami whispered, "I always believed Amanda was trying to do the right thing, but Em..." She gulped. "There may have been innocent people down there, I couldn't be sure."

Emily grimaced. If there were any people inside, the occupants would have been trapped. They would have met a grisly death by crushing. She tried to clear the horrid idea from her mind.

She leaned back on her heels as she digested the information. She knew that there had to be a good reason for Amanda's actions.

While only minutes ago, she had wanted Justin to return, now she checked the road again, hoping he would not. Emily didn't want him to find out about what had happened, at least not while Kiami was in such a state.

She thought about how well he had handled things after she allowed Jacob to take the gems. He had been cool and calm. Even supportive.

She chewed at her lip as she considered his transformation since the two girls had left.

It was true that he had come to terms with the way he had been acting. He had even apologized for it. Even so, there was no doubt in her mind that he would jump to conclusions if he found out that Amanda had collapsed an entire mountain that very well could have harbored innocent lives. After all, in the past he had threatened to kill her if he discovered that Aden was dead, even though he had barely known him at the time.

She didn't want him to revert to that state of mind.

Anger flashed across Emily's features. Bloise had told them to stay away; he had been adamant. "I'm not lecturing you, but you shouldn't have gone." She tugged at one of the curls that hung down in front of her face and twisted it tightly around her finger as she continued. "I need to think."

When she had first found the note in the castle library, it hadn't been the right time to reveal it. But she had known it would come in handy, so she had held on to it. In fact, she had taken the entire book to help conceal the fact that she had stumbled upon it.

With her mind made up, she jumped to her feet. It was time to show Kiami the letter. Something had changed between her and Amanda on the mountain; she could tell by the way Kiami spoke her name. It came out of her mouth sounding as if it was a bad word.

She raced up the stairs and pulled the book from beneath her small bed. She used her fingers to trace over the runes and sapling that had been carved into the cover before flipping it open. The folded sheet of paper was still there, nestled between two of the yellowed pages.

Emily collected it and skimmed its contents. The letter revealed Amanda's private thoughts and feelings. Like Kiami was now, she was obviously very troubled when she wrote it. It appeared to have been created after she had escaped with Aden from Jacob's control.

Whether Amanda was a hero or villain, Emily knew she could never really give up. None of them could. What would be the point?

She hoped reading the letter would help Kiami to understand, because since she had returned, Emily felt a pull to move on.

She understood that was why time had seemed to stop while Kiami was away. Now, the need tugged at her to begin her mission. She had to find the missing half-bloods. She would lead the search, and she would begin with or without Etzion.

Amanda had been right after all: she was a warrior.

And she was ready to move them forward.

## About the Author

**M. Ainihi** is a passionate Dark Fantasy Author, proud Mother, Wife, and Adventurer. Hailing from the wilds of Upstate New York and currently residing in the Chicagoland area, Endow is the third novel in a planned quartet.

# Also by M. Ainihi

**Rise: A Blood Inheritance Novel**
Most humans do not know about the existence of the outer realms, or the fierce battles that once waged between the magical races before their creation. But for teen Amanda, ever since she encountered the jinni in the forest, it's her new reality, a place where darkness lies around every corner, and she's lost almost all hope of surviving it.

**Lost: A Blood Inheritance Novel**
Before Amanda knew about the seven realms, she longed to know her mother. Now her inherited gift is the very thing she fears most, and even as she fights to keep her shadow magic at bay, she can feel it growing inside her...

**The Warning Signs**

Coming Soon...

www.ingramcontent.com/pod-product-compliance
Lightning Source LLC
Chambersburg PA
CBHW020417010526
44118CB00010B/293